The Catholic Church Saved My Marriage

A. David Anders

The Catholic Church Saved My Marriage

Discovering Hidden Grace in the Sacrament of Matrimony

EWTN PUBLISHING, INC.
Irondale, Alabama

Cover design by Perceptions Design Studio.

On the cover: Saint Peter's Basilica and Square in Vatican City, Rome, Italy; image courtesy of Sopotnicki/Shutterstock (482453902).

Nihil Obstat: Very Rev. Bryan W. Jerabek, J.C.L., *Censor Librorum*
Imprimatur: +Robert J. Baker, S.T.D., *Bishop of Birmingham in Alabama*
May 2, 2018, Memorial of St. Athanasius, Bishop and Doctor

EWTN Publishing, Inc.
5817 Old Leeds Road, Irondale, AL 35210

Distributed by Sophia Institute Press, Box 5284, Manchester, NH 03108.

Library of Congress Cataloging-in-Publication Data

Names: Anders, A. David, author.
Title: The Catholic Church saved my marriage : discovering hidden grace in the sacrament of matrimony / A. David Anders.
Description: Irondale, Alabama : EWTN Publishing, Inc., 2018. Includes bibliographical references.
Identifiers: LCCN 2018010816 ISBN 9781682780527 (pbk. : alk. paper)
Subjects: LCSH: Marriage—Religious aspects—Catholic Church. Catholic Church—Doctrines. Anders, David L.
Classification: LCC BX2250 .A542 2018 DDC 261.8/3581088282—dc23 LC record available at https://lccn.loc.gov/2018010816

To my parents,
Louis H. Anders Jr. and Marsha A. Anders,
my first great teachers in Christian marriage

Contents

The Catholic Church Saved My Marriage

Introduction

The Catholic Church saved my marriage and, quite possibly, my life. By the early 2000s, my marriage had degraded to the point at which I honestly wished for death. It was a matter not simply of incompatibility or conflict but of reciprocal contempt. No love. No affection. No mutual appreciation. My wife and I were held together only by the barest thread of duty to our children and a vow that I regretted with all my heart.

Today, I enjoy a life of marital bliss. We are in complete harmony on the most important issues of life, faith, and family. We delight in each other's company. We bear one another's burdens. We forgive each other's faults. We accept life's hardships—including the inevitable marital conflicts—as necessary steps in a journey of moral and spiritual progress. We have found that marriage is something bigger than both of us—infinitely bigger. Marriage, we have discovered, is a life of service, in which we strive to make our union into a sign and instrument of God's peace, justice, and love in the world.

We could not have gotten here without the Catholic Church. I am an adult convert to the Faith, and my wife is a revert. My initial interest in Catholicism was purely academic and had nothing to do with marriage, which I only gradually came to understand. As we began to practice the Catholic Faith and, later, to internalize the Church's teaching on marriage, the results were literally astounding. People who knew us before testify to the miracle that occurred in our lives. This book tells the story of that transformation.

I know that this message is controversial. I speak on a regular basis with Catholics and non-Catholics throughout the world about their objections to the Catholic Faith. I host the radio show *Called to Communion* for the EWTN Global Catholic Radio Network, in which we invite listeners to call in to explain why they are *not* Catholic. Catholic teaching on marriage and sexuality ranks very high on the list of reasons people reject the Faith.

The reason Catholic teaching is controversial is not hard to understand. Church teaching on marriage is so difficult that Jesus' own apostles found it hard to believe. Jesus taught that marriage is a permanent, indissoluble union of one man and one woman for life (Matt. 19:1–11). Furthermore, the Catholic Faith insists that we practice a kind of sexual restraint in marriage that seems unthinkable in today's sex-saturated culture. When Jesus expounded His doctrine on marriage, His disciples responded, "If such is the case of a man with his wife, it is not expedient to marry" (Matt. 19:10).

Catholic teaching on marriage includes some stark negative commands: no divorce, no contraception, no in vitro fertilization, and no sexual union that terminates in acts that are intrinsically infertile. Many people who encounter Catholic teaching for the first time are absolutely shocked by this rigor. They see the negative commands as something arbitrary, because they do not understand their *purpose*.

The truth is that the Catholic Faith offers an extraordinarily positive vision of married life. It does not ignore human happiness, sexual pleasure, joy, or intimacy. Rather, it sets those good things in a much larger context. By subordinating sex and pleasure to a much higher good, the Catholic Faith provides the means to sustain such intimacy for one's whole life.

I am convinced that few people today, even among Catholics, understand just how rich the promise of Catholic married life is. The Church offers much more than rules about sexual restraint; She offers a way to make marriage into something transcendent, even mystical. The Church sees Christian marriage as inseparable from the ends of Christian faith itself, and those ends are distinctly supernatural.

* * *

This book describes my personal discovery of the Catholic teaching on marriage and the beautiful effect it had on my life. Much of that teaching is applicable to anyone, Catholic or not. However, its most sublime elements cannot be accepted without vigorous embrace of the Catholic Faith as a whole. In my own journey, the full Catholic doctrine of marriage became credible only as I came to understand that larger vision of the moral and spiritual life. The text, therefore, is autobiographical but also apologetic. I offer a defense of the Church's most controversial teachings with reference to that larger vision.

Why doesn't the Church allow divorce and remarriage? Why does She oppose "gay marriage," abortion, and contraception? Why does She endorse such a strict vision of marital sexuality? There are good answers to these questions that apply to everyone, Christian or not. How can I bear an unhappy marriage? What value is there in suffering? How could I forgive grave offenses? What should we teach our children about the meaning of life? The Catholic answers to these questions can be lived only by the deep embrace of Catholic faith and spirituality.

In my own journey into the Catholic Faith, I was surprised to discover that the Church envisions a contemplative dimension to

Christian marriage. In Catholic thought, contemplation means having a deep, intuitive, almost experiential awareness of God through the life of prayer. Traditionally, contemplation has been the primary goal of monks and nuns, those called to dedicate themselves fully to the spiritual life. But the Church teaches that marriage is *also* a kind of full-time Christian spirituality, and one that offers a deep, interior experience of God.

Keeping this mystical dimension of marriage in view is absolutely necessary if we are to understand how to approach suffering in marriage. For many people today, the fact of personal pain would seem to justify almost any decision meant to relieve that pain. Are you in a difficult marriage? Then why not leave and try something else? Have you discovered that your sexual urges don't line up with the demands of heterosexual or monogamous marriage? Why deny yourself satisfaction? But the Catholic Faith teaches that such suffering can be supremely meaningful, leading even to a mystical union with God.

One of my major concerns in writing this book is to urge suffering couples to a vigorous practice of the Catholic Faith. My hope is that Catholic couples will discover new strength for their marriages and that non-Catholic couples will consider what the Catholic Faith has to offer. This is not a self-help book or a book of marriage and family therapy—such books can be good and useful and apply as much to the natural as to the sacramental marriage; rather, my aim is to point married couples *beyond* the tools of psychology or natural marriage and to help them embrace a transcendent vision of Christian conjugal life.

* * *

This book does not attempt to make a systematic and comprehensive case for the Catholic Faith. Anyone who would like to hear me offer such a comprehensive apologetic may investigate the many articles, podcasts, and archived videos I have made readily available online. Nor is this book a typical conversion narrative, insofar as I do not recount all the experiences, thoughts, or influences that led me to the Catholic Faith. Instead, I focus on how my discovery of the Faith challenged my understanding of the moral life, and of marriage and parenting in particular.

Much of the book concerns my transition from being a Protestant to a Catholic Christian. Even as I do not make a comprehensive case for Catholicism, I do not attempt to offer a comprehensive picture of the Protestantism I left behind. This may frustrate Protestant readers who feel I have misrepresented their tradition. In my defense, I understand that Protestantism is rich and diverse, and I have no intention of disparaging the entire tradition. Many of my Protestant friends are far more virtuous than I am and have not suffered my marital problems. I am only recounting my experience.

—Albert David Anders
Advent, 2017

Chapter 1

"I Hate You"

"I hate you," Jill said.

"That makes sense," I thought. "I hate me, too."

I sat in my small, gray house in Cahaba Heights, Alabama, just outside Birmingham, wondering how I got to this point. The floor was strewn with books and papers from my dissertation research. For several years, I had buried myself in the sixteenth century, studying the theology and history of the Protestant Reformation. Now, at the end of the twentieth century, that study was costing me my faith *and* my marriage. My wife looked at me with undisguised contempt.

"You don't do anything for us," she complained. "All you do is study. You don't have a job. We don't have any money. Our kids are sick all the time. You don't support us, financially or emotionally."

"What do you want me to do?" I asked.

"Quit your school," she said. "Go get a job. Get us money. It's the only thing that matters now."

The only thing that matters . . .

Those words stuck in my heart. How could my wife say that? When I met Jill, she was the most idealistic person I had ever met. She threw herself headlong into causes, charities, the arts, and, eventually, religion. She despised the workaday life. She had always encouraged me to "follow my bliss," wherever that might lead. But now here she was rejecting every scrap of meaning we had ever shared. All she cared about was financial security. Not even the affection of marriage mattered to her anymore.

The truth is, Jill felt abandoned. Emotionally, I had left her for the library. I worked long, long hours, leaving my wife and children at home while I pursued my professional interests. Financially, we were in pitiful shape after ten years of grad school with little to show for it. Socially, we were alone. I moved around the country, collecting degrees, but we failed to collect many lasting friendships. But the worst alienation was spiritual. We thought we shared a common vision of married life, but with work, children, and planning for the future, the pressures of life revealed major cracks in that common vision. We married as evangelical Protestants and were committed in principle to lifelong marital fidelity. Only slowly did we come to realize that this was not enough to unite us.

The truth was that I also felt abandoned. Initially my wife supported my academic interests. Now, only a few months from my earning my Ph.D., she was asking me to throw the whole thing away. And it's not as if I had a viable alternative: Job prospects for people with an "almost Ph.D." in religion are slim. I keenly felt the loss of her affections, and I didn't understand why small conflicts had started to erupt so fiercely. Spats about housekeeping or childcare masked deep, enduring hidden tensions.

That day in Cahaba Heights, my mountain of books and papers seemed suddenly worthless in light of the sober realization: "I have lost my wife."

I was in despair. It seemed I had thrown away my life. As my wife seemed to be slipping away, so did any possibility of warmth or intimacy. Our only point of contact was our children, and even then we were often at odds about how to parent them. I was determined to do the right thing for my kids—but I was looking at a life of quiet, hopeless, meaningless pain. And, though Jill did not fully realize it, I was also losing my Protestant faith. With that loss, my dream of teaching Protestant theology was evaporating as well. *Secretly*, I hoped one of us would get hit by a bus. (I didn't care which one.)

* * *

How did I end up here? It seemed impossible that my life would come to this. I grew up in the Protestant South—in Birmingham, Alabama—and my parents were devout, conservative Presbyterians. Strong marriages ran in our family, at least on my dad's side. My mother's mantra was "Murder, maybe; divorce, never!" I never heard my father utter a word of criticism about my mother. Every meal was "the best-tasting food I ever put in my mouth." My mother suffered an abusive childhood, but my father's family was stable, and so their commitment to each other supplied everything my mother had lacked growing up—unconditional love, acceptance, and mutual respect. I always assumed I would follow them in their marriage, and in their religion.

Jill's childhood was more like my mom's. Her father was distant, and her mother suffered from a severe personality disorder, alcoholism, and chronic depression. Like many people with personality disorders, Jill's mother was prone to "splitting": She divided the world into "good people" and "bad people," and the categories could shift rapidly and unpredictably. If you happened to fall into the "bad" category on any given day, you would be the target of horrific verbal abuse. It could appear anywhere and at any time. For instance, the family might be dining at a restaurant when suddenly Jill's mother would begin screaming profanity at her children, and the rant could last *for hours*. That was my wife's formative childhood experience.

We met in a French class at Tulane University in 1990. Jill was *really* cute, a tiny thing with long, thick brown hair and hazel eyes. She spoke French well—was nuts for it, in fact. (She once told me she'd rather be a French cat than an American person.) She journaled endlessly, and she didn't give a fig for superficiality. "Do what you love" was her motto: passion before practicality; art, not artifice. Unsurprisingly, then, she was an aspiring actress. Her motto could have been "Give me theater or give me death."

I, on the other hand, was coming off a high school experience of adolescent rock bands, wild partying, cheap flings, and teenage rebellion. I was looking for more in my life, and Jill seemed to fit the bill perfectly. Here was a serious and intelligent girl who was neither a tease nor aloof. We shared an interest in foreign cultures. She seemed to like me—and it didn't hurt that she was beautiful.

We began to spend time together speaking French, drinking coffee, taking long walks, and riding elephants at the New Orleans Zoo. We also passed many hours lolling about under the Spanish moss and the oaks of Audubon Park.

One afternoon in the spring of 1990, under the New Orleans moss, we had an experience that I will never forget. As we sat there in the grass, Jill began to unfold her past to me. That day in the park I learned that her serious side was more than literary interest or cultured detachment: It was born of deep and profound suffering. Her mother was abusive. Her emotionally distant father shared his wife's alcoholism, smoked heavily, and was dying of cancer. Death, disease, abandonment, and dysfunction had followed her extended family for generations. Her life was one of chaotic, unremitting emotional torture.

Oddly enough, Jill's family was Catholic: Her uncle is a well-respected Catholic scholar, and her father was a regular Mass goer. Even her mother had received the sacraments at some point. But Catholicism meant next to nothing to the family: They never discussed religion, and the Faith provided absolutely no moral compass, no solace, and no way to cope with their suffering. By the time Jill made her Confirmation, she was a confirmed atheist.

I saw very clearly that day under the moss that this girl had a gaping hole in her heart so big that no man could fill it, least of all me. I saw, more clearly than ever before, that only God could meet a need like this. Religion wasn't worth a dime if it couldn't speak to this kind of suffering. I decided I had to try to bring God's love to this need, and so, for the first time in my life, I saw Christian evangelism as something more than a rote religious duty. I cared about this girl and wanted to help her. God—whoever He was—and God's love—whatever that meant—had to come to this girl.

All my life I had heard countless preachers talk about life on the skids and the joy of those who find God's love. I had listened to endless testimonies of those who had been abused, broken, addicted, and incarcerated and who had found redemption in the gospel. I can't say that these narratives conformed to my experience, but they were deeply embedded in my psyche. If God could help these people, surely He could help Jill.

There was something eerily prophetic about that day in the park. As Jill narrated her past, I caught a glimpse of the future. I saw our lives potentially bound together through the mystery of suffering, and reshaped through the mystery of redemption. I felt that the universe was giving me a choice: Will you embrace suffering and redemption, or will you shelter yourself through the pursuit of pleasure? Up to that point, I had lived for pleasure and I didn't know what a life of meaning would look like. If I had known what was coming I probably would have said no. I'm glad now that I didn't know.

I began sharing with her about Protestant Christianity, the tradition I was raised in. Much of what I said was rote—a formula I had heard for years, but one I believed with sincerity. "Tell God you're sorry for your sins. Pray for forgiveness. Ask Jesus to come into your heart. Then God will forgive you and give you a new start on life. You'll be 'saved,' your place in Heaven guaranteed."

What Jill was thinking at the time, I don't really know. She told me later that I seemed "safe" to her. She also said there was something strangely attractive about my faith in God. And so she followed me to a nearby Presbyterian church.

My own spirituality at the time was hardly mature. I had lived a wild life in high school and only recently decided to reform. I made very gradual progress in morality, with many setbacks. My behavior toward women was less than honorable. I thought myself improved, though, simply because I had returned to church and had given up partying. I still had much to learn about humility, charity, patience, and chastity.

Despite my own poor example, Jill took an interest in the Presbyterian church. She also taught me much about charity and service: At her urging and with her help, I took up tutoring in an inner-city school. Together, we were stumbling toward the light. One day, again at her urging, we went to hear a missionary speak about his life of Christian service in a poor Central American community. His obvious love for the people and his belief in God's love were infectious. I had heard many similar talks in my life, but for Jill it was a first. She was hooked: "That's what I want," she said. "I want to give my life in missionary work, in service to God and neighbor."

What happened next seems almost surreal in retrospect. Jill prodded me insistently to approach the man about his work and to ask what it would take to join him. The pastor was shocked, I'm sure. Who were these two nineteen-year-old college kids asking to come to Latin America? "Look," he said, "this is a lifetime commitment. You've got to have training. You've got to raise financial support. You should at least have finished Bible college." Jill turned to me and said with finality, "I'm going to Bible college."

This is where common sense should have kicked in. I had grown up with Christian missionaries all around me, so I knew how the thing worked. In Protestant communities, a select few rise from the ranks to join full-time Christian missionary work. They usually have a strong Christian tradition in their family or have had a dramatic conversion—something so psychologically compelling that they cast aside societal expectations to embrace a radical Christian life.

In Protestant churches, the missionaries are like Catholic monks or nuns. They stand out as icons of discipleship for all the rest. After years of faithful service in the local church, they get tapped (or volunteer) for this higher life. Then follow years of seminary training and the arduous process of raising financial support, which can take just as long. Some people prepare ten years before venturing out into the field. And here was this girl, who didn't know the Old from the New Testament, who couldn't have told a Baptist from an Episcopalian, telling me and the world that she was ready to jump in with both feet. And what did I say? "I'll come, too."

What was I thinking? Why would I throw in my lot with this girl in what was obviously a fool's errand? I barely knew her: We had been dating for less than a year. And in that time, I learned that she had a psychotic family, was chronically depressed, and was prone to making manifestly rash decisions. Why would I volunteer to come along? Looking back, I now understand that deep down, I yearned for the absolute. I had no intention, really, of going into Christian ministry, but I saw in a flash that Jill's rash decision had just a scintilla of sanity about it. The thing to do—which we all have to do—is to find the meaning of life and embrace it.

There is a Buddhist story about the teacher Bodhidharma, who was on retreat in a cave for many weeks when a man came to him, seeking instruction and enlightenment. The teacher, however, refused to speak to him. Finally, in a fit of agitation, the man cut off his own arm and presented it to Bodhidharma as proof of his sincerity. I think that story captures something of what I was feeling. "This may be the dumbest thing I've ever done, but I see that I've got to do *something* like this."

Eventually we settled on Wheaton College in Wheaton, Illinois, as our base for our new lives. Wheaton is a bastion of both conservative Protestant enthusiasm and academic respectability: A large number of graduates go on to earn Ph.D.s in various fields, and alumni are heavily represented in the faculty and the leadership of prominent Christian ministries and schools. (The school's most famous graduate is the late Billy Graham.) The students are mostly serious about their religion and their studies, so it seemed an excellent place to grow in our newly shared faith.

Two things of enormous importance happened to us at Wheaton. The first is that I began the academic study of theology with very intelligent, faithful Christians. Rational investigation of the faith utterly captivated me. My previous education had been very fragmented; I had mastered individual subjects but had no deep engagement with *reality as a whole*, no systematic investigation of ethics, morals, or the nature and meaning of human life. But here at Wheaton, I encountered the notion of a philosophical and religious worldview—the discipleship of the mind and learning how to *think* like a Christian. I decided my mission was to give my life to the study of theology.

Jill, however, was initially disillusioned with school. Unlike me, she took no special pleasure in academic theology, since what she really wanted was mysticism and not religion from a textbook. She grew so discouraged that she thought of going back home to New York. Frightened of losing her for good, I made another big decision (bigger by far than the decision to study theology): I asked Jill to marry me. She accepted and decided not to go back to New York.

Together we finished school quickly by taking summer classes. We made a few friends but spent most of our time together. I studied very, very hard and made good grades. We began to plan for our wedding and for what we thought would be a life of Christian service.

* * *

We married in Birmingham, Alabama, in a Protestant wedding, and we immediately began to worship at a Pentecostal church where we were exposed to a type of Christian worship that was much more exuberant than anything we had known before. We both found jobs while we settled into marriage. It was a time of great religious fervor and great spiritual friendships, but after a year we were keen to move the plan forward. I enrolled at Trinity Evangelical Divinity School in Deerfield, Illinois, in 1993.

On the drive from the Deep South to the Midwest, I got my first hint that all was not right. We talked about seminary and our plans, and I spoke with enthusiasm about my impending theological studies and pursuing a career in academia. Jill turned cold.

"I thought you wanted to go into ministry," she said.

"I do want to go into ministry," I assured her. "I want to go into *teaching* ministry."

"But you want to go into *pastoral* teaching, right? Into missionary work?"

There it was. Jill was still envisioning cross-cultural ministry. She had a romantic notion of abandoning the comforts of American civilization and launching out into the unknown depths. We had continued to meet missionaries over the years, and she remained deeply attracted to that idea.

For my purposes, I had developed a vision just as romantic and idealistic: I became intoxicated by the idea of theology. At the time I was unfamiliar with the medieval notion that theology was the Queen of the Sciences, but I would have wholeheartedly embraced it. For me, theology had become not so much a tool for pastoral ministry but a way of becoming abstracted into a kind of Platonic reverie.

What each of us wanted, in our own way, was something transcendent. We were looking for an experience of God that was more than a mere formula, something that could take us out of ourselves. Our Pentecostal experience gestured toward that by engaging deep emotion in the act of worship. But Jill wanted more. She wanted to fly away to another world, and I wanted to withdraw from the world intellectually. There was enough overlap in our verbal affirmations of faith to keep the conflict between those two spiritualities largely hidden from us. But the cracks began to appear on that trip to Illinois.

At Trinity, we found a wonderful community of like-minded people. Most of the young couples who were training for ministry were going into pastoral work. Some were studying counseling, some missions, and some, like me, were preparing for academic theology. Most of the students were men, while the wives worked on campus in the library, in the admissions office, or in other departments. Jill worked in admissions.

We spent two delightful years at Trinity, and even though we never managed to find a church we loved, we had so many friends on campus that we never felt the lack. But Jill began to feel another lack: *childlessness*. There were many young women around us having children while their husbands studied for ministry. Jill caught the bug and began pressuring me for a baby. We conceived our first child, Jonathan, who was born at the same time I graduated, May of 1995.

Looking back on it now, it seems almost incredible how little we discussed parenthood, childbearing, or even the meaning of marital sexuality. Until we conceived Jonathan, we practiced various forms of contraception. Sex seemed like a good, licit, marital leisure activity, but it was essentially disconnected from childbearing. The decision to have children meant making a real decision to *stop* contracepting. It would be years before I understood how hurtful and wrong my attitude toward sex and fertility was.

What is the purpose of marriage? What is the purpose of marital sexuality? How is marriage related to one's service in the Church, or one's relationship to God? Our answers to these questions were inchoate and poorly formed. As Protestant Christians, we were strong on the idea of marital fidelity—the idea that one should save oneself for marriage and remain faithful to one's spouse. But our understanding was incomplete. I thought nothing of seeking sexual intimacy with my wife while putting off her desire for children.

Once Jill asked me, "When will you be ready for children?"

"When I'm done with school," I said.

"When will that be?" she inquired.

"I don't know," I answered. "Maybe in six or seven years. Maybe ten."

When I proposed marriage, we never discussed the timing of children. We talked only in terms of our future Christian ministry. And so I felt that *I* was the one following the original game plan, and *she* was the one deviating from our unwritten agreement. I couldn't understand why this made her feel used.

The time at Trinity was formative. I received good, broad exposure to the sources of Protestant thought: biblical languages, Scripture, Church history, and theology. I was blessed to study with great models of Christian scholarship. But above all, I imbibed the deep anti-Catholicism of my professors. Ironically, I am grateful for that emphasis. My professors forced me to consider the main historic areas of disagreement between Protestants and Catholics. Without that study, it is unlikely I would ever have become Catholic.

* * *

In the fall of 1995, I enrolled in doctoral studies at the University of Iowa, where I focused on religious history with an emphasis on the Protestant Reformation. Graduate school was very different from seminary. My interest in friends and community collapsed while I plowed into study with a kind of desperate obsession. My aspiration was to become the greatest scholar I could possibly be, and so any moment I wasn't studying seemed like a moment lost. I became physically agitated if I became separated from my books—like modern teenagers and their smartphones. I rose early, lived in the library, and stayed up as late as I could manage. My dissertation would eventually stretch to almost eight hundred pages; my bibliography alone was almost a hundred pages.

Jill's experience of Iowa was comparatively barren. Unlike our life in Illinois, there weren't any seminary wives to befriend, and she had little in common with the female graduate students. Jill's interests turned to motherhood, not Greek or Sanskrit, and we had our second child (Joshua) in 1997 and our third (Zoey) two years later.

Our church life remained a problem. We visited many congregations—Baptist, Presbyterian, Pentecostal—and we even settled for a while on a Korean congregation. (Church suppers were a delight since I love kimchi!) But close friendships remained elusive.

It's unsurprising to me in retrospect that cracks began to appear in our relationship. The birth of children, the stress of parenting, the isolation and loneliness, and my prolonged absence started taking their toll on Jill. The Iowa weather didn't help either: From fall to spring we were usually buried in snow and trapped indoors. Jill's past traumas began to reappear in her psyche, and her emotional state descended into depression. Conflicts over housekeeping and childcare gradually took on a more acrimonious character. We were far from open warfare, but persistent irritation was common.

With marital stress, I withdrew more and more into my studies. The more I studied, however, the more difficulties I found with my Protestant faith.

Jill knew nothing about my theological struggles. I did not fully realize them myself, since much of what troubled me was beneath my conscious awareness. My main preoccupations, instead, were finishing my doctoral degree and managing my wife's deteriorating emotional state. As we approached our fourth year in Iowa, I knew I had to change something.

I was fortunate to receive a dissertation fellowship from the University of Iowa, which gave me a year with no responsibilities except writing. Free to leave the university campus, I thought a change of location might help Jill. If we returned to Birmingham, I could work on my dissertation and she could access our old circle of Pentecostal friends, which I thought might help with her depression. I shared my idea with Jill and she embraced it enthusiastically. In May of 1999, we packed our things into a rental van and put our three children in the car and drove to Alabama. How badly my plan would fail!

Relocating to Birmingham taught me the truth of the old maxim "You can never go home again." Our first stay in Birmingham had been with a warm, supportive community of vibrant Christians, but we returned to find that the old leaders had left, married friends had divorced, and young students had moved on to professional life. We failed to connect with new friends and found the failure of old relationships to be very disheartening. Furthermore, suburban Birmingham was more expensive than Iowa. We were the only starving graduate students in a world of rising young professionals. Far from relieving our marital stress, moving to Birmingham increased that stress to the breaking point.

I had thought Jill would thrive in comfortable and familiar circumstances, but instead they forced her to come to terms with what marriage was costing her. Initially, marrying me had seemed like a way out of her painful past. Cross-cultural ministry had been her romantic dream for something distant and exotic. Graduate school always kept alive the promise of that "something more" because everyone around us had been in transition, but in the sleepy suburbs of Birmingham, people weren't preparing for something else. They were getting on with life.

Suddenly, Jill realized that *this might be her life!* She was married to an aspiring academic who would always be in a library or a classroom, and who would never have enough time for her or her children. He had no money. He would always be in transition. A frantic job search would follow graduate school. The battle for tenure would come next, followed by the struggle for full professor. There would be articles, books, lectures, and then retirement. Meanwhile, she would be stuck in a suburban home raising children alone. The workaday world had caught up to her by surprise! Where was the hope? Where was the transcendence? Where was the sense of belonging to something eternally significant?

Jill's depression sunk to new lows. At the same time, my children began to get sick—constantly sick. The low point came when two of our children were hospitalized with pneumonia at the same time. My eldest, Jonathan, languished for days in a feverish delirium, and we had to resort to surgery to draw infectious fluid from his lungs. Meanwhile, his baby sister, Zoey, lay in a hospital crib with an IV stuck to her head. I spent the dawn of the new millennium—New Year's Eve, 1999—in the hospital with two desperately sick children.

The stress was almost more than Jill could bear. She felt as if she had no part in my academic work, and our church life had fallen apart. Since our kids were sick so often, she coped by throwing herself obsessively into the pursuit of physical health. Everything was sterile. She watched the kids' diet and exposure to toxins, and she religiously avoided anyone with even a hint of infection. But I did not share her intense, laser focus on sickness and health, which I felt was overzealous. From that point on, she began to regard me with suspicion and distrust.

I worked on my dissertation, but I also pursued my private theological speculations. I investigated Catholic theology, including moral theology, and more and more I was struck by the simple but compelling logic of natural-law thinking. The moral good is determined by the nature of human persons, and not simply by an arbitrary divine command. Martin Luther King Jr. famously appealed to this idea in his "Letter from the Birmingham Jail."

As a Protestant, I thought morality was delimited by the express words of Scripture. If the Bible didn't condemn a particular action, then that action must be acceptable. But Catholic thought forced me to question this idea. Weren't there many moral questions that Scripture didn't raise directly? Applied to questions of human sexuality, this line of thinking could have some stark consequences—as I would soon discover even more fully.

For our whole married life, we had practiced some form of contraception. Now I began to question that decision. The turning point for me was an article I read by a non-Catholic physician detailing scientific research on birth control pills. I learned that the pills are potentially abortifacient, meaning they can cause the death of newly fertilized zygotes, and that they can also be harmful to mothers. While there was a lot more I had to learn about contraception, this article provided sufficient evidence for me to decide, at least provisionally, against it.

Jill was aware of none of this. Until I suggested that we should stop using contraception and pursue natural family planning, the idea of not using birth control had never occurred to her. This struck her as a perfectly arbitrary demand from a husband who couldn't be bothered to provide even the most basic financial and emotional support to her and her family. Worse, it came out of precisely the studies that had alienated me from her. I was over-thinking things, she asserted, with no concern for her or her body.

To Jill, it was just another one of David's private fancies, like a theological fetish. Far from making her feel loved and respected, the request made her feel used and objectified.

"I hate you."

Chapter 2

What Is Marriage?

What is marriage? I am sure neither my wife nor I ever asked that question before becoming Catholic. People were getting married around us all the time, and it seemed clear enough: Men and women take vows, live together, and usually have a family. As a Protestant Christian, I also believed that you should save yourself for your spouse, that divorce was impermissible, and that husbands and wives should be faithful to each other.

Jill had few settled ideas on marriage. She knew only that she did not want to repeat her parents' experience, and so she adopted most of my Protestant notions of marriage without objection. But apart from a few well-defined prohibitions, neither of us had any clear notion of what marriage *was for* or how it should be ordered. Our childhood experience of family life was far more important to shaping our attitudes than any explicit religious doctrine.

Differences in temperament, personality, and values led to difficult tensions in our marriage, but they need not have led to disaster. Our marriage broke down because we did not have a sufficiently robust, shared vision of married life. A vague sense of being man and wife and a few negative commands were not enough to strengthen us against marital conflict. Nor was our shallow spirituality enough to help us recover from deep emotional wounds.

* * *

"Dad, will you pray for something for me?"

"Sure, son. What do you want?"

"Will you pray that Katherine falls in love with me?"

The first time I remember speaking to my father about sex and romance, I asked him to get me the girl of my dreams. I was thirteen years old.

"Yes, son. I'll pray she falls for you."

My parents had signed me up for ballroom dancing classes. When they were in school in the 1950s, every young person could dance; in fact, there were dances to attend just about every weekend. In their minds, traditional dance was something every decent young person should know, and I was agreeable to the idea. After all, girls were increasingly interesting to me, but the girls at my school weren't all that reciprocating. Perhaps things would be better at dance class?

Katherine stood out from all the others. I think I never spoke more than ten words to her, but I was completely smitten, delirious, dizzyingly infatuated. What did I really want? I could hardly have told you. That she recognize me, accept me, marry me? It was my first real experience with the madness of "love."

I love and respect my father more than any other man on earth. Any shred of decency I have is because of him. I suppose he didn't want to break my heart, but I wish he hadn't acceded to my request. Couldn't he have let me down gently?

What do I wish he had said?

"Son, girls are great. I hope one day you meet an awesome young lady, marry her, and raise a family. But now is not the time. It's natural you should feel this way. God *made you* to feel this way. But what you're experiencing are *feelings*, and feelings aren't everything. The feelings will be there when the time is right, whatever girl you marry. But the time is not right. Enjoy the class. Dance with pretty girls. Learn to be a gentleman. But put off falling in love."

My father once told me, "I hope you kiss lots of girls. But save sex for marriage." The message I absorbed was this: The Bible draws a line around *coitus*. Sexual intercourse is to be saved for marriage, but everything else that makes up human sexuality—romance, infatuation, even pregnancy and children—can be disconnected from that act without ethical significance.

I learned two other things about sex and romance from my mother. When I was fairly young (grammar school age), my parents drew me aside to explain that mom was going to the hospital for a day or so. She was having a little operation that would make it so that she could not have any more children—a tubal ligation. At that age, I understood the basic biology of reproduction, but up to that point I didn't realize people would be sexually active without intending children. My mother's sterilization taught me that children might be an *unwelcome* side effect of sex. (I also remember feeling cheated. I mourned the loss of the siblings I would never know.)

The second thing I learned from my mother was a lesson in marital sexual ethics. She told me what her Presbyterian pastor had told her: Nothing is off limits between spouses, provided there is mutual consent. Protestants hold to the idea of *sola scriptura*: The Bible alone is our sole authority for moral or theological issues. There is no need to consider what reason, experience, or tradition can teach us about marriage and sexuality, and so, if the Bible does not explicitly condemn it, it must be inbounds.

The effect of all this on a young man was powerful. As near as I can tell, no one ever told me to tame, moderate, or master my sexual impulses. Date lots of girls. *Kiss lots of girls*. The only rule was to delay intercourse until marriage. Thus, my early instruction encouraged adolescent fantasy. Contraception seemed to remove the consequences of sexuality, and marriage made all things lawful.

In other respects, my education in marriage was more sober and inspiring. My parents set a wonderful example of love, fidelity, forgiveness, and tenderness. Truly, they are my heroes. They were completely committed to the indissolubility of marriage. My father talked many men out of divorcing their wives. Regardless of circumstances, he always gave the same blunt advice: "You may not do it. It is immoral." My parents' fidelity to marriage is the single greatest gift they ever gave me.

But what happens when Christians *do* get divorced and remarried? Our church had no good answer. Sometimes the divorced would get a nominal slap on the wrist, but then the impotent admonition: Do your best to keep the *second* marriage from falling apart.

* * *

When Jill was ten or eleven, she asked her mother, "Mom. What's a period?"

"It's the dot at the end of a sentence."

"No, mom. It's something else. I know it is. The girls at school are talking about it."

"No, Jill. It's the dot at the end of the sentence. Nothing else."

My parents did their best to educate me about sex and marriage, and what I lacked in moral instruction was not their fault, but the fault of their tradition. But Jill's experience was completely different. Her family did not talk about sex, fertility, bodies, or marriage. All that was seen as shameful and dirty, and thus completely off limits.

Jill had no positive example of romantic love. Her parents' marriage was loveless, unromantic, and bitterly acrimonious. There were drunken fights and screaming. There was no positive communication of any sort. At best they shifted between open warfare and shaky armistice. They intended to divorce until Jill's father was diagnosed with terminal cancer. To my mother-in-law's credit, she did remain married to him until his death.

It goes without saying that Jill had no religious or moral instruction in sex or marriage at all, except that she knew that her parents' example was pathological. Even so, she *wanted* them to instruct her, but they showed no interest at all, even when predatory males began lurking around her. They left Jill entirely to fend for herself.

Unsurprisingly, then, Jill developed conflicted feelings about marriage and sexuality. On the one hand, she wanted love, intimacy, trust, and commitment, and these things were vaguely connected to sex and marriage in her mind. On the other hand, she was deeply suspicious of sex and marriage. After all, her only positive examples came from popular culture, theater, and film—not exactly bastions of traditional morality.

* * *

What did the Christian faith contribute to my understanding of marriage? And how did I experience Christianity as a child? For me, evangelical Christianity was simply the way the world works. I could no more have questioned it than I could question gravity. In that faith, the Bible is God's word, given to us so we might learn the way of salvation. That plan of salvation is simple: God created mankind in His image, but man fell into sin. By faith in the death and Resurrection of Jesus, men can be reconciled to God, forgiven their sins, and reborn into a new life. The ultimate destiny of the saved is to spend eternity with God in Heaven.

That is the outline of my childhood faith, but there were other details that were very important for my youthful conception of married life. The first was our view of the Bible in relationship to Christian morality. Simply put, I believed that we discover absolute moral norms simply by reading the Bible. If Scripture clearly commands or prohibits something, then it is obligatory or forbidden. If Scripture is silent about something, then it is permitted.

Another important implication of my childhood faith was the clear delineation between "the saved" and "the lost." There is a children's song circulated in summer camps and Bible schools that goes like this: "One door and only one and yet its sides are two. I'm on the inside. On which side are you?" That offers a good depiction of our worldview. It also explains why we heavily emphasized *proselytism*. The line that runs through humanity is not one that separates the *good* from the *bad* but rather one that separates the saved from the damned, believers from unbelievers.

This leads to my final point about evangelical Christianity. I have known many heroic and charitable Evangelicals; indeed, many of them are far better people than I imagine I will ever be. But their religious anthropology frustrates attempts at moral heroism. Evangelical doctrine affirms the inherent and ineradicable corruption of the human heart. Martin Luther taught that men can be saved by faith alone. Why? Because even with the help of God's grace, people cannot stop sinning. Our lives are so saturated with pride, lust, sloth, and greed that our every thought remains hateful to God.

All of this had a very definite impact on my experience of marriage. I learned that extramarital sex is wrong and that divorce is wrong. But I also learned that morality is *essentially* rule following. Scripture commands or forbids, and we comply (or at least try to). I learned that efforts at moral living will ultimately and inevitably be frustrated. There may be clear rules of behavior, but the human heart is irreparably weak. Finally, I saw proselytism as a major component of Christian service. We praised those who wore themselves out in evangelism, even traveling to the farthest corners of the earth. But what of their children?

* * *

Looking back, it is not surprising that our marriage broke down. Though we shared the Christian faith, we lacked a well-articulated vision of married life. What is the purpose of marriage? What is the purpose of marital sexuality? What place do children and family have in marriage, in the Church, in Christian ministry? We almost never discussed these things. We married hoping for love, intimacy, and even a life of religious purpose. The problem was that we did not have a clear idea of how to achieve these things.

The early days of our marriage were enriched by our common excitement about our new life, our new church, and our new friends. We had our share of arguments, sometimes rather vehement, but we managed to forgive and forget. We turned toward one another for emotional and physical intimacy, and we looked forward to a life of Christian ministry.

The major cracks began to appear with our disagreements over the relative importance of children, family, and career. Necessarily, this also involved questions about contraception and the purpose of marital intimacy. Delaying children because of school had to mean using contraception, didn't it? What other option was there?

Outwardly, we had no philosophical disagreements. Jill would have verbally assented to my way of thinking: Contraception is good, and a casual approach to sex is good. But Jill began to value things differently. She ceased to value intimacy disconnected from children and family, and so she began to turn to me romantically *for children*. As I now realize, her intuition was correct. It was more real, more grounded in the nature of things.

For my part, I continued to pursue academic achievement with an obsessive fury. I loved my wife and children, of course, but I had a way of assimilating them into my intellectual vision of Christian ministry. To be honest, I used theology as a justification for my selfish pursuit of glory. I wanted to dominate intellectually and spiritually. I wanted to be significant.

To illustrate, I taught a class for the youth at our Korean Baptist church in Iowa City. I was a popular teacher, and I got a good deal of satisfaction out of my students' approval. Every Sunday, Jill would wait patiently for me to teach while she chased our two-year-old son around the church. I thought nothing of asking her to make that sacrifice week after week. I was *doing ministry*, after all. What could be more important? When she expressed frustration one week, I let her know that teaching this class *was my religious duty*, and it was her duty to support me. Her angry response rather took me aback.

My academic view of Christian life also affected my view of parenthood. I tended to value my children's intellectual formation to the exclusion of almost everything else: I had idealistic notions about raising little prodigies, as well as a very doctrinal view of religious instruction. I had almost no understanding of the need for the formation of character, of habits of virtue, or of what psychologists now call *emotional intelligence*.

For her part, Jill stressed the physical health and safety of the children. Given her chaotic upbringing, she also knew little about character formation. As I pulled away more and more into my career, Jill turned more and more to the physical needs of her children. Each of us began to feel challenged by the other's priorities.

Jill once told me about a dream she had that symbolized our growing divide. A river passes right through downtown Iowa City, so you have to cross a bridge to get from one side of town to the other. In her dream, I was standing with my back to the river, oblivious to what was behind me. Meanwhile, she was watching in horror as the water swelled to a mighty tidal wave bearing down on the bridge. "David," she said, "I'm afraid to cross the bridge." "I'm not worried about that at all," I replied. While I spoke, the bridge was swept away in the torrent.

"I'm not worried about that at all." That was my standard, dismissive response to nearly all her queries. No matter what her concern, she could expect that retort. It didn't matter how important it was to her.

At the same time, I tried occasionally to reach Jill with *my* concerns and interests. It didn't go over well—and in retrospect I can see why. To this day, few things are guaranteed to put my wife to sleep like the question, "Can I tell you about a book I'm reading?"

Gradually, we turned to each other only to make demands and to have our needs met rather than for mutual love, encouragement, or true intimacy. Each of us began to feel used and exploited. I felt that Jill valued the children over and above me, and that she exploited me for my paternity and labor. Jill felt taken advantage of both physically and emotionally. And yet, during all this time, we had no *overt* disagreement about the nature or purpose of sex, marriage, children, parenthood, faith, or Christian spirituality. Our disagreements were more *felt* than thought or expressed.

These unstated disagreements bred suspicion and distrust. In pain and confusion, we turned away from each other—Jill to the kids, me to my books. We became defensive and shut down emotionally. Ultimately, we fell into mutual contempt.

Marriage therapist John Gottman has identified what he calls "The Four Horsemen of the Apocalypse" for marriage.[1] These are the descending steps that most couples go through before ending in divorce or despair, and we recapitulated these steps almost perfectly.

The first step is when conflict slips over into criticism. Conflict is not the problem; any two people living together will have conflict. But conflict doesn't have to escalate to criticism of the

[1] John Gottman, *Why Marriages Succeed or Fail: And How You Can Make Yours Last* (New York: Simon and Schuster, 1994), 68.

person. "Please don't leave your socks on the floor" may signal a conflict over housekeeping. "You obviously don't care about me because you always leave your socks on the floor," on the other hand, is criticism.

The next step is defensiveness. Fearful of criticism, we strike back to protect ourselves: "Oh, yeah? Well, if you didn't keep the house such a mess, maybe I'd know where to put my socks!" This is followed by emotional withdrawal. Tired of the pain and the criticism, we pull away from each other. According to Gottman, the *husband's* emotional withdrawal is more frequently associated with marital breakdown than the wife's. Wives tend to stay more emotionally engaged, even if negatively.

Finally, there is contempt, the greatest predictor of divorce. "I hate you."

* * *

Two foundational problems led to the breakdown of our marriage. The first was philosophical: We thought we agreed on marital ethics, but we lacked a truly comprehensive understanding of marriage. We both believed marriage was a divine institution, indissoluble and inviolable. But what was marriage *for*? Exactly how was it related to our Christian faith?

And the second fundamental problem in our marriage was a lack of virtue. The best ethical philosophy in the world is of little value if you can't live it. Patience, kindness, love, wisdom, forgiveness, and sacrifice are needed in abundance in order to have a good marriage. And we were woefully deficient.

* * *

When Jill said, "I hate you," I didn't know what to do. We had had fights before—she had even thrown her wedding ring at me—but this was different. This was not a passionate outburst, but the cold, determined rebuttal of someone who had made up her mind. I could sense the finality of her rejection.

The days that followed were the worst in my life. Jill brought up divorce more than once, and she strongly suggested separation. It felt like a knife plunged into my heart over, and over, and over again. But again, and again, and again, I refused to consider either option: no divorce and no separation.

There were two reasons I absolutely refused to consider the possibility of divorce. The first was my absolute horror at the word. I thank God with all my heart that my parents gave me the conviction that marriage is sacred and divorce an unthinkable abomination. To divorce my wife would have been to fracture my soul at the foundation. I would truly rather have died. In fact, part of me wanted to die to escape this dilemma: "Please God, let me get hit by a bus!"

The other reason I refused to divorce was my children. There was just no way I was going to step away from my kids, and I knew Jill felt the same. Whatever conflict we experienced to that point was nothing compared with the battle that would ensue over the lives of our children.

I once asked an attorney who handled both criminal defense and divorce cases if he was ever afraid to defend murderers, rapists, and other serious offenders.

"Oh, no," he said. "Often, you are the only person supporting the accused and they are genuinely grateful. What really scares me are the divorces. You wouldn't believe how vicious these people can get."

That is where I sensed we would go if we divorced. It would be World War III. It would be better just to die.

What, then, could I possibly do? I had one final trick up my sleeve, but it failed miserably.

"Jill, will you come pray with me?" I demanded.

"No."

"What do you mean, no? You must. Come do it now."

"No. I won't. I won't pray with you."

I was overbearing and desperate. I was demanding. She would have nothing to do with me, in prayer, or in any other way.

The problem is that I didn't really want Jill to pray with me, at least not as I would come to understand prayer. What I really wanted was to leverage the power of religious sentiment. I wanted to manipulate her. I could not bend her to my will, so I demanded that she yield to me emotionally in the context of prayer. Today, the memory disgusts me.

How could I be so deceived? How could I not see the blackness of my own heart? In Catholic tradition, prayer is so much more than simply asking God for things. With God's help, prayer is a battle against ourselves. Prayer is where we cast off self-deception, artifice, pride, and egotism. Prayer is where we learn to stand naked before God and transparent to ourselves. Prayer is where we take up the Cross of Christ, allow ourselves to be slain, and entrust our resurrection to God alone.

Did I want Jill to pray with me that day? Not at all. How could I? I knew nothing about prayer. All I knew was how to demand my own will in God's name, to gratify my own maudlin self-pity with what I thought were religious sentiments, and to clothe my hubris sanctimoniously with the mantle of "faith."

I knew nothing about real prayer because I rejected the wisdom of Christian tradition and the transforming power of grace. All I needed was "faith alone," my own individual, self-sufficient, cocksure "faith." At the heart of my failing marriage, I had wrapped up and baptized my sins and vices in a religious veneer.

Chapter 3

Are Catholics Christians?

For the first twenty years of my life, I knew almost nothing about the Catholic Faith — only the stereotypes and caricatures of my anti-Catholic culture. Catholics were objects of pity or ridicule and targets for proselytism and conversion. They were certainly not subjects of moral insight or spiritual wisdom.

Study and experience challenged those prejudices. Through college, seminary, and graduate school, I began to learn that Catholics could be deeply insightful, virtuous, rational, and clear-headed — and even that the Church taught ideas and fostered moral attributes that I needed, but in which I was sorely lacking. Through study, the Church began to challenge me to reexamine my previous philosophy of life.

* * *

"Did you grow up a Christian?"

"Oh, no! I grew up Catholic!"

In my church when I was growing up, this was a common exchange. My family attended a large Presbyterian church with a very pronounced sense of its mission to bring everyone to personal faith in Jesus. We knew that Catholics did not have this kind of faith, and so we actively proselytized Catholics—and when they came to our church, it only reinforced our conviction that they didn't really know Jesus. Many truly did not have a living spirituality until they came to us, and they often complained about their Catholic upbringing.

In my youth, then, the only Catholics I knew were ex-Catholics, and they all told the same story about their exodus from the Catholic Church: "I didn't know Christ, and I didn't know Scripture." It was very easy to believe Catholicism had nothing to offer. I also learned very early that Catholics were profoundly superstitious. This was the impression I got from my mother, who was a Spanish instructor at a local university, and from her Latin American Protestant friends. She loved cross-cultural studies and traveled to Central America, Mexico, and Spain. My mother witnessed Latin American Catholicism up close, but all she could see was the worship of statues, devotion to Mary, and what she imagined were self-abusive penances. Her ex-Catholic friends told similar stories.

My mother told me often about the Mexican Catholics who would crawl to the Shrine of Our Lady of Guadalupe on their knees. It is hard for me to express how much she despised this devotion, and I shared the revulsion. These stories typified for me everything that was wrong with the Catholic Church.

And so, when I met Jill, I was sure I knew all I needed to know about the Catholic Church. Catholics were ignorant, superstitious, and immoral. They were slavishly obedient to a tyrant, knew nothing of God's grace, lived in craven, neurotic fear of damnation or purgatory, and tried to crawl their way to heaven by mindlessly repeating empty rituals.

Needless to say, I had no Catholic friends as a child, and I had no Catholic teachers or mentors. All the literature I read was anti-Catholic, even in my secular high school and college. The first time

I considered the Catholic doctrine of the Eucharist was when I read about it in James Joyce's novel *A Portrait of the Artist as a Young Man*—hardly a sympathetic portrayal. History classes depicted the Catholic Middle Ages as corrupt and backward, and my college and seminary professors viciously attacked Catholic theology.

It took at least ten years and countless hours of reading, studying, and praying for me to revise my views on the Catholic Church. I also began meeting people who challenged my stereotypes about Catholicism. Some of those people were Catholic, but not all of them; some honest scholars with no interest in Protestant-Catholic debates also prompted me to reexamine old prejudices.

* * *

I began my college studies in 1989 in New Orleans, where I found, generally speaking, two kinds of students: alcohol abusers and engineers. There may not have been a greater pool of unused talent in the country than the group of young people who populated uptown New Orleans. Most of the students I knew were intelligent but ridiculously unmotivated; their dorms were saturated with sex and alcohol. My brilliant roommate would sleep *for days at a time*—through class, through meals, and through conversation—only to rouse himself and go off again in search of diversion.

I had one friend, Dave from Dallas, who was different. He was as fun-loving as the rest of us, but he always seemed to keep his pastimes in their proper place. He'd have a beer, smoke a cigarette, and shoot pool, but I never saw him overly intoxicated. He didn't take any girls home, but he wasn't a prude, either. I never heard him offer a word of criticism: When my roommate passed out in broad daylight, Dave would just laugh.

Which is why I was so surprised when I saw Dave get angry. We were walking down the hallway of our dorm when Dave looked at a flier that had been posted on the wall. I don't remember the specifics, but it had something to do with a university-sponsored colloquium on sex. Suddenly, Dave erupted and tore the thing from the wall. "Why?" he yelled. "Why *does everything here always have to be about sex*?" He turned red and stomped off, slamming his door behind him. I stood there dumbfounded: It was the first time I ever heard a young man object to too much sex. And then I thought about that crucifix that Dave always wore around his neck.

Dave didn't talk much about his faith, except to praise his Jesuit high school. "You can't imagine how cool these guys are," he would say of his Jesuit teachers. "They smoke; they drink; they dance. But they love God." You would think that the best thing about Jesuit education was to have drinking, smoking teachers—until that day in the hall. Dave was the first person to show me a different side of Catholicism. For Dave, being a Christian was not about holding yourself aloof in ritual purity, or proselytizing your benighted neighbor. It was about being real and seeking authentic happiness for as many people as possible.

Dave was no Puritan. He didn't judge people, and he wasn't a sappy, self-absorbed ascetic wrapped up in his own spirituality. Dave was flesh and blood: He had a sense of humor, and he was passionate about life. What motivated his frustration with our sex-saturated dorm, I suspect, was not prudishness, but rather his understanding that these New Orleans hedonists were taking all the joy out of sex. Seminars on technique and technology reduced sex to mere mechanics and body parts and removed the *human beings*. Dave loved *people*—real people, who could love and laugh and live. People, to Dave, were more than sex organs.

* * *

"The Catholic Church is a special world. A very special world," my professor announced.

"What does he mean?" I thought. It was a strange way to start a lecture.

Professor Dwight Bozeman was not a Catholic. As far as I know, he didn't practice any religion. But he was an exceedingly honest scholar, a brilliant man, and an engaging teacher. He delighted in the peculiarities of religious faith: He could draw you into lengthy disquisitions about the idiosyncrasies of New England Puritans, Shakers, Mormons, Muslims, Buddhists, or Baptists. He had a knack for figuring out what made them tick.

In a course on American religion at the University of Iowa, Professor Bozeman decided to introduce Catholicism with a text from the *Code of Canon Law* on the training of seminary students. It was another strange choice. Why not the life of a saint or a theological text? He read aloud:

> Students are so to be formed that, imbued with love of the Church of Christ, they are bound by humble and filial charity to the Roman Pontiff, the successor of Peter, are attached to their own bishop as faithful coworkers, and work together with their brothers. (245.2)

"It should strike you," he said, "how different this is from what you would read in a Baptist seminary. The Catholic priest is to love *Christ's Church*. What would you expect from Baptists? 'Seminary students should love Christ.' But here we find 'the love of Christ's Church.' The Church, for a Catholic, is a divine reality, the presence of Christ in the world. Roman Catholicism is different. It is a special world. A very special world."

I was puzzled: How could you love an institution? Like so many people, I thought of the Catholic Church only as the embodiment of bureaucratic, hierarchical corruption, and so I always assumed Catholics were either deluded fools or abusive manipulators. But Bozeman, as usual, had placed his finger on the key point: The

Catholic Church sees Herself as the living embodiment of Jesus, as Christ's real presence in the world. "Whoever beholds the Church," said St. Gregory of Nyssa, "beholds Christ."

That day in Iowa was the first time I ever really thought about the true mystery of the Church in the Catholic Faith. How could something *so human*—so full of incompetence and flesh and pride and ambition—be the living presence of God in the world? The idea was absurd. But then my thoughts wandered back to Dave, the first Catholic I ever really respected.

I caught a glimpse of something I had never seen before. Salvation isn't just about going to Heaven when you die, escaping the world, or simply having a personal relationship with Jesus. It's about *being Christ in the world*, embracing life with both hands, and raising it all up with as many people as possible in transcendent joy. "Whoever beholds the Church beholds Christ." That mediocre priest, that baby, that grandmother, that college student, and even that corrupt medieval pope: Could God be present *in that*? Could a man love *that*?

Dave and his beloved Jesuits were a clue for me. Being Catholic—being Christ in the world—doesn't exempt you from flesh and blood, even from ambition, pride, and sin. But it makes you a sign, like that crucifix around Dave's neck. It's a life visibly marked out by and for transcendence. Maybe you won't reach that transcendence. Maybe you spurn the gift. Maybe, God forbid, you do something horrible. But, being Catholic, you've been joined to a family set apart for more than empty pleasure. It's not just an otherworldly club, either. You are part of a family called to authentic happiness in this life *and* the next. Could a man love that? Yes, I believe he could.

* * *

"You know the Catholics are right about justification."

"What's that, you say?" I couldn't believe my ears.

"I said, the Catholics are right about justification."

When I arrived in Iowa, I was dead set against Catholicism, and the heart of my rejection was the doctrine of justification, which answers the question, "How are we made right with God?" Of all the things we had against Catholics, this one seemed to me to be the clearest in Scripture. St. Paul said, "Man is not justified by works of the law but through faith in Jesus Christ" (Gal. 2:16). How can you get clearer than that? But the Catholics argued that we are saved by grace through faith *and works*. I didn't see how the Catholics had a leg to stand on.

There was another graduate student at the school who was a New Testament scholar. I didn't know him well, but I knew he had a Baptist background and had gone to a conservative seminary. I thought maybe we could be friends and ideological allies, until one afternoon, when I met him on the stairs of Gilmore Hall. As we struck up a conversation, I learned with horror that he had lost his faith. Critical scholarship on the Bible, he said, had destroyed it. But he wasn't bitter about it—mostly he was melancholy.

"You know what bothers me?" he asked. "It's how much I love my children. I look at them, and I want our relationship to last forever. I don't ever want to lose them. But I have no hope of Heaven. I don't think it's real. When we die, that's it. I'll lose my children forever."

I choked with sorrow at the thought. "My wife still goes to the Methodist Church," he continued. "The pastor believes. I envy his faith."

What struck me about my friend was his humble honesty. Many former believers are embittered, but my new friend didn't look back at his years as a believer with anger or resentment. He had no agenda, no ideological motive; he simply stopped believing.

As a "good" Evangelical, I thought I should at least try to share something of my faith with him. I began to tell the story of my own conversion, my relationship with Christ, my prayer life, and my hope of salvation in the forgiveness of sins. It had a distinctly Protestant ring to it.

"I've heard that before," he said. "But, you know, it's really the Catholics who are right about justification."

I startled, unable to take in what he said. This fellow was no Catholic, so he had no dog in the fight. He wasn't even a believer. Why would he deny the obvious? It was the first time I'd ever met an intelligent, well-informed student of the New Testament who took the Catholic view.

"How do you mean?" I asked.

I knew the Bible very well. After seminary, I could explain the content of every chapter of the New Testament from memory. But my friend knew the text better than I did. He knew the underlying Greek texts, and he knew all the Protestant arguments. And then, right there in front of me, he began to take them apart piece by piece. He walked me through Scripture in a way that made more sense than anything I had learned in my years under the tutelage of hard-core Protestants.

In brief, he explained that the Catholic Faith says that Christ came to bring love, and that we need saving because we don't love. We are alienated from God, from each other, and from the deepest needs of our own hearts. "To be saved" means to be transformed in love, to be reconciled to both God and neighbor. The Church is the living sign of that love in the world. It's God's plan, says Scripture, to reconcile all men "through the Church" (Eph. 3:10).

But what about justification by faith?

He quickly answered my question with a question: What did that actually mean for St. Paul? In his day, Jewish Christians insisted that Gentile converts should obey the Mosaic Law and that we are "justified"—that is, declared to be in the right—by following God's law. But Paul responded that the Law of Moses was only for a time and that the true heart of the law was the command to love (Rom. 13:8). It's not Jewishness in an ethnic or legal sense, but being Jewish "at heart"—committing to a life transformed by charity—that makes one a real disciple. And that charity comes to us by faith (Rom. 2:25–29).

For Catholics, he continued, one begins the Christian life not so much with a new set of rules (the law), but with faith in Jesus Christ. Jesus lived a life of extraordinary self-sacrifice, even to laying down His life. God raised Him from the dead, and He invites us to share in that power in a mysterious way. "We were buried ... with him by baptism into death, so that as Christ was raised from the dead by the glory of the Father, we too might walk in newness of life" (Rom. 6:4). The whole thrust of Paul's letters is that rules and laws don't make men good. *Love* makes men good. And we receive that love through faith in Christ. It is "poured into our hearts through the Holy Spirit" (Rom. 5:5).

Catholics agree with Protestants that we could never earn or deserve the happiness of Heaven, *if we were left to our own devices*. But the Good News is that God pours His own love into our hearts through faith. Through the gift of grace, we really can and do love God and neighbor. We really are transformed in love. God doesn't save us *in spite of* our sin but rather by *healing us* from sin—by really transforming us in to vessels of love and mercy. We are saved by grace alone, yes, but it is a grace that "works" in our lives.

I knew the Catholic position from seminary, of course, and I knew how to refute it. So I challenged my new friend: Isn't love *a work?* If we are saved by love, doesn't that mean we have to *do something*? Our conversation became quite technical, as I trotted out some fine distinctions and theological jargon. But he stayed one step ahead of me. Each time I made an objection, he answered it calmly and thoroughly.

That day in Gilmore Hall, I met the first person I ever knew who made a rigorous, knowledgeable, persuasive case for the Catholic interpretation of Scripture. I was not totally convinced, but I was unnerved. In the months and years to come, I plowed more deeply into the Scriptures, the best biblical commentaries, the history of the early Church, and the writings of theologians. To my chagrin, the Catholic position became increasingly credible. The point of Christian faith is to transform us in love. Without that, we are not really "saved" at all. If anyone says he loves God but hates his brother, John tells us, then he is a liar and the truth is not in him (1 John 2:4).

* * *

I found another clue when our department welcomed a Catholic ethicist as a visiting scholar. His name was James Gaffney of Loyola University of New Orleans, and he also accepted an invitation to address the whole religious-studies community on a controversial topic: the ethics of abortion. I liked a good academic fight, so I went out of curiosity and hope, I suppose, for a bit of blood sport.

The lecture was another important stepping stone on my journey to the Catholic Faith—precisely because of the absence of Catholicism from the lecture. Professor Gaffney made no appeal to Scripture or to Sacred Tradition. From reason alone, he argued for the objective value of unborn human life.

Gaffney surprised me by refusing at the outset to engage in political discussion. The talk was not to be about political advocacy but rather moral theology. Gaffney confessed that he found pro-life politics impractical because he didn't believe it was possible to legislate successfully against abortion. We might dispute this, of course, but his lack of political interest noticeably lowered the emotional temperature in the room. Instead, Gaffney asked a simple question: Is it possible to say meaningfully, "When I was a fetus"?

He drew our attention to a basic moral intuition: The Golden Rule presupposes that I can imagine myself in someone else's situation. "If I were in his shoes," we ask ourselves, "how would I like to be treated?" There are conditions in which this question makes no sense; for instance, I cannot imagine myself as a stalactite. But it is perfectly intelligible to imagine oneself as a fetus because, in fact, I *was* a fetus. Therefore, it makes sense to ask, "How would I want to be treated if I were a fetus? Would I want to be aborted?"

Gaffney followed this argument with several others, including the principle of reasonable doubt. If we don't convict a criminal when there is a reasonable doubt of his guilt, then should we kill a fetus if there is even a reasonable doubt about its status as a moral object? He also appealed to the medical evidence. When someone's heart and brain stop, we say he is dead. What should we say about a fetus who *has* heart and brain activity? Shouldn't we take that as evidence of life? If not, why not?

In the question-and-answer period after his talk, I listened, dumbfounded, as a young woman explained that he had changed her mind. She went to the talk favoring abortion and left believing abortion to be objectively immoral. I think it was the first time I had ever seen someone change their fundamental moral convictions, on the spot, in response to argument.

Not everyone was convinced, of course. One feminist professor argued for the absurd thesis that the right to life depends on having had quality experiences. Adult humans have rights that fetuses lack, she held, since they have had such experiences and fetuses have not. The horror of her position struck me immediately. Who are you, I thought, to decide whether my experiences qualify me to live?

Several things impressed me about the afternoon. First, I was surprised that a Christian ethicist could argue effectively without recourse to Scripture. I grew up in a tradition that did not have much place for philosophical ethics or natural law. Our default move was always to appeal to Scripture. But, truth be told, I had never known anyone to change their moral viewpoint in a heartbeat simply because "Scripture says so."

Second, the way Gaffney knocked his audience off balance by foreswearing politics was effective and impressive. He did not advocate a controversial policy; instead, he argued for a theoretical conclusion. The result of that discretion was that he won a hearing, at least from one young woman.

Third, Gaffney's discussion helped expose the vacuity of the opposition. Though he said he was not arguing for a political conclusion, it was obvious to me that many of his detractors were arguing directly from political conclusions they wanted to reach rather than from first principles. They were rationalizing a political program instead of seeking truth.

This episode got me thinking about the Catholic tradition in a new light. My Protestant professors had said we can know nothing to be true apart from Scripture. One of my professors was Carl Henry, the founder of *Christianity Today*, cofounder and president of the National Association of Evangelicals, and perhaps the most influential evangelical theologian of the mid-twentieth century. He once wrote, "Reason loosed from revelation cannot know any normative reality."[2]

During my time in Iowa, I was increasingly finding the opposite to be true: Revelation, without reason or tradition, produced chaos. Furthermore, it's simply not true that reason alone has no access to moral realities. There are basic moral values that are almost universally shared. The atheist psychologist Martin Seligman has identified at least six ethical values found in nearly every culture

[2] Carl Henry, "Natural Law and a Nihilistic Culture" *First Things* (January 1995).

throughout history, and sociologist Donald E. Brown has identified hundreds of human universals, both ethical and philosophical, found in every culture.[3] There are many moral truths we can know apart from Scripture.

Today, I can't help thinking about Professor Gaffney's lecture when I remember the time I first told my young daughter about abortion. "Why would anyone do that?" she asked me. "*They* wouldn't want to have been aborted." I laughed when I realized what this meant: It took a Ph.D. ethicist to teach me what even a little child could know.

* * *

Over the four years we spent in Iowa, I gained a deeper appreciation for the depth and wisdom of Catholic tradition. I read hundreds of authors and many thousands of pages of Christian theology. While my focus was on the history of Protestantism, I did not ignore Catholic writers. Instead of the superstitious half pagans I had been raised to expect, I found Catholic saints to be men and women of extraordinary holiness and erudition.

My first great teacher was St. Augustine of Hippo (354–430), who wrote the greatest spiritual autobiography in history, his *Confessions*. Through Augustine's eyes, I discovered the Church as a living body, united across time and space by the connective tissue of sacraments, joined in a transcendent vision of divine love. Augustine taught me that physical signs (the sacraments) were not obstacles to a deep interior life, but rather were objective, visible evidence of God's promise of salvation. Augustine rescued me from

[3] Martin Seligman, *Authentic Happiness: Using the New Positive Psychology to Realize Your Potential for Lasting Fulfillment* (New York: Atria Books, 2004); Donald E. Brown, *Human Universals* (New York: McGraw-Hill, 1991).

my Protestant individualism and introduced me to a Catholic vision of Christian unity.

Augustine challenged my view of the Christian past. As a Protestant, I always thought that the early Church was theologically pure and that false doctrine corrupted Her during the Middle Ages. In Augustine, however, I found a fully developed, robust Catholicism. He taught the primacy of love and denied "faith alone." He described the authority of reason, Church, and tradition *together*, instead of "Scripture alone." He rejected the bare literal or "fundamentalist" view of the Bible. He acknowledged the important role of the saints and their relics. He saw the sacraments as real means of grace, rather than empty symbols. From Augustine, I learned I could no longer claim continuity with the Christian past if I remained a Protestant.

The next Catholic writer to shake me up was the Jesuit theologian John Courtney Murray (1904–1967). Murray was famous for his political theology, in which he reflected on the American Constitution and situated it in the Catholic natural-law tradition. He was also an important voice at the Second Vatican Council, especially in drafting the statement on religious liberty, *Dignitatis Humanae*. His book *We Hold These Truths* was a watershed in my intellectual development. Murray taught me that Catholics have a profound tradition of rational reflection on social and political questions, and he opened my eyes to the beauty of the Catholic philosophy.

Catholics see the Church as a beacon in world history. The Church is not simply a spiritual aggregate of people who believe in Jesus; rather, She is a historical subject, an actor on the world stage. She sows seeds of transcendence throughout culture: the dignity of the person, the freedom of the conscience, the integrity of the intellect, the importance of human rights, the essential equality of men and women, and the ideals of forgiveness, reconciliation, and peace. These are Catholic ideas without clear precedent in pagan culture. They began to flower right when I was taught the corruption had infected Her, in medieval society, with tangible effects on culture and government. Murray opened my eyes to the profound and benevolent influence of the Catholic Church on human history. Things I took for granted as an American patriot I began to see I owed to the Catholic Church.

While in Iowa I discovered a third Catholic writer who deeply impressed me: the Trappist monk Thomas Merton (1915–1968). Before Merton, I had a relatively shallow understanding of Christian spirituality. I had glanced at the Catholic mystics but understood very little about them. I just couldn't make sense of someone like Teresa of Avila: Her *Interior Castle* seemed like nonsense. But Merton was a man of prodigious literary talent; indeed, his *Seven Storey Mountain* is one of the great works of American spiritual autobiography. He also had a gift for explaining the contemporary significance of mysticism. By reading Merton, I began to wonder what I might be missing if I stayed away from the Catholic Church.

I grew up thinking that prayer was largely petitionary: "Dear God, can I please have . . . ?" Catholicism, by contrast, has a rich and diverse tradition of reflection on prayer. While petition certainly is one purpose of prayer, the ultimate end of prayer is union of the soul with God in love. The tradition that studies this interior transformation is called *mystical theology*. Though there are Protestants who have emphasized the interior life, there is nothing in Protestantism quite like the Catholic mystical tradition, and it was Merton who first opened my eyes to this treasure.

Today, my list of favorite Catholic authors is much longer: I would now have to place St. Thomas Aquinas at the head of the list, along with John Henry Newman and Joseph Ratzinger (Pope Benedict XVI). Hundreds of lesser luminaries have also rounded out my faith. But in the early years, just a few Catholic writers and a handful of acquaintances began to unravel my childhood prejudices.

* * *

Are Catholics really Christians? Can they be saved? We treated such questions with the utmost seriousness in my Protestant background. The consensus was that Catholics were certainly not Christian *precisely in virtue of being Catholic*. Catholicism itself was a grotesque corruption of Christian faith, which, if followed seriously, could lead only to ruin. There might be a few Christians scattered among Catholic parishes, but they were Christian *despite* their Catholicism, not because of it.

Prejudices can be easy to maintain because they are often founded on partial truths. To make matters worse, confirmation bias heavily skews our perception of the world. We see what we expect to see, and what we want to see. If you want to see Catholics as ignorant, superstitious, credulous, and corrupt, there is plenty of evidence for that conclusion. Indeed, I have been Catholic now for almost fifteen years, and I have learned that some Catholics really are ignorant, superstitious, credulous, and corrupt—just like many, many other people in the world.

But that is not the whole story. Catholics are also noble, self-sacrificial, intelligent, wise, and profound—and these traits are not accidental to their Catholicism. Through their Catholic faith and because of it, Catholic men and women have pushed back the boundaries of ignorance and hate across time and across the globe as the light to the nations that Christ called them to be. Along the way, they also produced a tradition of wisdom unparalleled for its sophistication.

Cardinal Francis George, the late archbishop of Chicago, appreciated the depth and uniqueness of this tradition. He wrote:

> The Full Body of Reflection on the truths of the Catholic faith represents the collected wisdom of intelligent and holy men and women from every part of the world over two millennia. Its tributaries include thousands of years of ancient Jewish experience as well as the cultures of Mesopotamia and Egypt; it draws on the entire heritage of classical Greece and Rome, the civilizations of the Middle Ages, the Renaissance, the Enlightenment, the scientific revolution, romanticism, modernism, and our globalized postmodern culture. Briefly put, there is nothing quite like it.[4]

To put the matter quite bluntly, I grew up as an anti-Catholic bigot—a narrow-minded, cocksure, stupid bigot. I barely understood my own tradition, let alone the depth and riches of the Catholic Faith. Bit by bit, kind, intelligent people challenged my prejudices and slowly introduced me to the possibility that I did not know everything and that I had something to learn from Catholics.

Academic interest and intellectual curiosity inspired most of my early learning about Catholicism, but life experience also played a role. As my marriage and family progressed and the responsibilities of adulthood continued to press, I came to see that the settled answers of my childhood were unsatisfactory. Previously, I had a simple view of religious life: Believe the Bible and pray to receive Christ. Study revealed that my naïve understanding of Christian faith was contrary to history, to reason, and to the Bible, and experience proved it was also wreaking havoc in my life. Life by "faith alone" was driving me into a moral quagmire from which only the Catholic Faith would save me.

[4] Cardinal Francis George, OMI, *A Godly Humanism: Clarifying the Hope That Lies Within* (Washington, DC: Catholic University of America Press, 2015), 1.

Chapter 4

Life by "Faith Alone"

I once got into a full-blown theological debate about the reliability of the Bible with a friend of mine who was an unbeliever.

I felt that I was quite prepared for the debate since I had recently read *The New Testament Documents: Are They Reliable?* by the outstanding evangelical biblical scholar F. F. Bruce. I raised point after point in what I thought was a stunning performance, and my friend was ill-prepared to answer my position intellectually. But his response floored me.

"Dave," he said, "I don't like Christians."

What had I expected? Did I think he would convert to Christianity just because I had read more books on New Testament manuscripts? Instead, he was just disgusted with the whole procedure. "Christians are just arrogant blowhards who force their beliefs on everyone else." I was hard-pressed to deny it. Indeed, I recognized that this was an accurate description of my own character.

Thomas à Kempis, the author of *The Imitation of Christ*, once wrote that it is pointless to debate brilliantly about the Trinity if, by being an arrogant ass, you are displeasing to the Trinity. That is the Catholic point of view. It does not matter if you have the most brilliant theology in the world unless your thinking is grounded in a rich appreciation of other people and their inherent value.

"You know," I thought, "I don't like Christians either. At least, I don't like them when their religion makes them into arrogant bores." My religion made me into an arrogant bore. Worse, it justified behaviors I would not tolerate in anyone else in any other realm of human activity.

Marriage, family, and life experience forced me to realize how sterile and vacuous my theology was. When I got married, I thought I could get along on faith alone and Scripture alone, but gradually, I came to doubt it. More than just Scripture, I also needed the practical wisdom of tradition. And more than just faith, I needed a faith that works through love.

* * *

"Could you do me a favor?" I asked.

"No! I'm sick of those words! I don't ever want to hear you say that again!"

I stood in the kitchen of our little rented duplex in Iowa City. I was stunned. Where had that angry response come from?

It was time for me to go to work. (It always seemed to be time for me to go to work.) Jill would stay home with little Jonathan and baby Joshua. As I gathered my things that day, the state of the kitchen annoyed me: I wanted things one way, and Jill wanted them another. On the way out the door, I mentioned a domestic detail I wished she'd change. "Jill, would you do me a favor?"

Jill and I grew up in very different homes. My mother was obsessed with neatness and efficiency. Everything had to be in its place; everything had to look nice. Nothing was to be wasted, and towels were to be reused until they were stiff.

In Jill's home, sanitation, cleanliness, and fresh smells were valued. My mother-in-law used to spray all her beds with Lysol every morning. Towels were thrown on the bathroom floor after one use in order to mop up excess water and to be deposited in the wash.

It was inevitable that we would clash over housekeeping, even more than we would clash over childrearing. For Jill, children should be kept clean, bundled up, and safe from germs. I thought boys should tumble around on the floors of nurseries. Jill would buy only the most expensive, organic baby food. I thought they were all pretty much the same.

These kinds of differences are, in their proper perspective, trivial. They certainly don't have to provoke an emotional crisis. Today, Jill and I still differ over domestic policy, but we don't fight about it. We've learned to accept our differences. But that day in Iowa was a different matter. I had taken to pointing out all the little things I wanted to be changed whenever I saw them, always *on my way out the door*.

* * *

Jill's experience of Iowa was very different from mine. While I lived a life of academic contemplation, secure in the library or in the office for teaching assistants, Jill spent her time caring for children, often buried under piles of snow. In our small duplex, she felt anything but secure.

We shared a front porch with the occupants of the other half of our duplex, which meant we frequently passed our neighbors coming and going. We never kept the same neighbors for very long. Some we liked very much and had over to dinner, but others were more difficult.

Two women, whom we'll call Sally and Beth, moved in one day. The very day they arrived, Sally and Beth knocked at our door—and they looked and smelled of alcohol.

"Would you watch our kids?" they asked.

"What?"

"We're meeting some men," they answered. "Would you watch our kids?"

Jill and I were not very discerning when we were younger, and we got taken advantage of sometimes—but we weren't falling for this.

"I don't think so," I said.

As you might expect, the next few months were interesting and confounding. Three little kids wandered to our house quite regularly, looking for food.

"Do you have any bread? Any eggs?"

Sally and Beth were gone. The kids were alone with nothing to eat.

Occasionally, we heard screaming and threats of violence. Jill came home one day to find a man sitting on our shared front porch. We learned he was recently released from prison and that he had some relationship to one of the kids. Jill began to feel afraid.

While Jill stayed home next to the ex-con, I went to work in Gilmore Hall, where I shared an office with half a dozen teaching assistants. My life was taken up with medieval philosophy, Puritan social history, and fourth-century theology. I ran from teaching to writing to library research. It took the trunk of my car to return my library holdings every six months.

For half the year, the snow fell and the temperature dropped, and so we mostly stayed indoors. I sat with my colleagues in the ivory tower. Jill held down the fort a few miles away with two baby boys, Sally and Beth, their hungry kids, and the ex-con on the porch. From me, she heard mostly two things: "I've got to study" and "Could you do me a favor?"

* * *

"I'll be waiting for you in my office when you are ready to start class."

I'll never forget those words as long as I live.

Graduate studies in theology require knowledge of several languages. At the University of Iowa, graduate courses in Latin and German were taught by Dr. Trudy Champe. I remember her as an incredibly sharp, fair, and demanding teacher. She was an Austrian Catholic with a good command of the Catholic tradition and a strong independent streak. We rarely talked religion, but I remember that she was always respectful toward my Protestant faith. I suspect, in retrospect, that she found it mildly amusing—except one day when she was distinctly annoyed.

At that time of my life, my mantra was still *sola fide*—"faith alone." Buried to my neck in Protestant dogmatics, I was keenly committed to this rallying cry of the Reformation. In my evangelical mind-set, "faith alone" meant I should urge people to personal conversion through "the sinner's prayer."[5] Meanwhile, my college and seminary professors stressed the importance of "worldview evangelism," which means challenging the philosophy of nonbelievers and arguing for the intellectual superiority of Protestant faith. When you put those two convictions together—proselytism and "faith alone" conversion—it's not hard to see how I could be a bothersome dinner guest.

My language courses were very small, with only a few students, a teaching assistant, and Dr. Champe. One of my fellow students was a philosopher, and so one day, before Dr. Champe arrived, we struck up a conversation about a technical point in the history of philosophy. Now, in my mind, any theoretical question was a prelude to "worldview evangelism." Every person I met was a potential convert. This gave me a sense of privilege and an air

[5] There are many versions of this prayer, but it usually goes something like this: "God, I know I am a sinner. Please forgive my sins. I accept Jesus into my heart. Amen."

of importance. Whenever I shot off my mouth, I felt I was doing "the Lord's work."

Well, I was doing "the Lord's work" when Dr. Champe came in. Pretty taken with myself and caught up in my important task, I failed to acknowledge her. She stood there quietly watching me until finally, exasperated, she said, "I'll be in my office when you are ready to start class."

Her words cut through me like a cold blade. In an instant, I saw myself as if from the outside, and I wasn't an evangelist but a boorish oaf. I took off after Dr. Champe, filled with remorse, and found her in her office.

"I'm so sorry," I said. "I was rude. Please forgive me."

I don't remember what exactly she said, but I know she was hard on me at first. Gradually, the extent of my superficiality dawned on me. I began to see other areas of my life where I fell short. My attachment to study and, frankly, to vanity were the real culprits. I could not see my own insensitivity because I hid behind the concepts of "ministry" and "theology."

The doctrine of *sola fide* was of real help in furthering this self-deception. The only thing that matters, I thought, is the content of one's belief system. Not only do works not save us, but they are as useful as filthy rags. The most important thing I could do—more important even than treating my friends and family with respect—was to shore up that belief system with strong arguments.

My professor's rebuke struck me harder than I even would have expected—and certainly more than she expected. Deep remorse flooded me as I considered how I failed my family in the name of my self-centered "studies." Tears came to my eyes, and I said again—to Dr. Champe, but also in a sense to my family and friends—"Please forgive me. I'm sorry."

That day in Dr. Champe's class, I realized that my religion was making me a jerk and a bore. I was far from becoming Catholic, but subconsciously the logic of the Catholic Faith began to work on me. I needed much more than forgiveness or "faith alone": I needed qualitative, *sanctifying* change in my life. From that day forward, I discovered a new openness to the Catholic Faith. When I investigated the sacraments, sanctifying grace, and the lives of the saints with an open mind, I saw something I desperately needed.

And I learned one other thing: Stop what you are doing and say hello when someone walks into a room!

* * *

"If you died tonight, do you know for sure that you'd go to Heaven?"

In 1962, Presbyterian pastor James Kennedy authored what is perhaps the best-known evangelism training program in the Protestant world, called Evangelism Explosion. The heart of the program consists in two "diagnostic questions" that evangelists are supposed to ask potential converts. The first is the more important: "If you died tonight, do you know for sure than you'd go to Heaven?"

The question captures what is perhaps the most important theological commitment in Protestantism: the conviction that a man can *know for sure* that he will go to Heaven when he dies—that a man can enter a state of life *today* that guarantees his salvation *in the future* and that he can know this fact with certainty.

If this is true, it would mean that there is literally nothing a man can do that will dislodge him from the path of life once he has entered it. It also means that his conscience, infallibly assured of salvation, should be immune to argument or persuasion to the contrary.

The basis of this conviction is not objective evidence that can be rationally evaluated, but rather a subjective judgment about one's own inner life. The Lutheran Augsburg Confession puts it like this: "Men ... are freely justified for Christ's sake, through faith, *when they believe they are received into favor*." In this tradition, believing that I am saved *makes me saved*.

Can you imagine any realm of human culture *other* than religion where we would encourage such attitudes? "Because I believe this to be true, I know with certainty that it is true, and nothing you say can persuade me otherwise." When we meet people like this in society, they tend to be, unsurprisingly, bores or ignorant blowhards. This attitude becomes even more dangerous in government, where people with this attitude are called ideologues—and they are often dangerous.

I am certainly not saying that all Protestants are bores or ideologues. Indeed, many are people of discretion and virtue, far more so than I. I am speaking, rather, about the dogmatic commitment that lies at the heart of the tradition, the logic of which worked on me such that I became a bore and a blowhard. And through my studies, I learned that I was not alone.

* * *

I trained as a specialist in Reformation history because I had been raised to believe that the Protestant Reformation represented a high point in the Christian tradition. As far as I was concerned, Martin Luther and John Calvin were the two most important theologians in Christian history; my pastors and teachers constantly treated them as the great forefathers of our religion. I was convinced that studying their lives and writings would offer the best possible intellectual foundation for my Christian faith. And so I spent years and years of my life on this project, during which I read tens of thousands of pages of their work, hundreds of biographies, and innumerable articles, unpublished manuscripts, letters, sermons, liturgies, treatises, and court records.

But I was coming to realize how the Protestant understanding of grace, assurance, faith, and salvation obscured my awareness of myself. Protestant teaching asserts that *everything* we do is sinful, but *everything* is forgiven—if we are "saved." This is not a doctrine that encouraged me in critical self-examination or growth in virtue. By focusing so heavily on my general depravity, sinfulness, and inability to save myself, I felt strangely freed from responsibility to root out individual faults.

In studying Luther and Calvin, I found, however, that my experience was not unique. John Calvin was a man who confessed the sinfulness of humanity but was incapable of confessing his own personal fault. In tens of thousands of pages of material by and about him, I do not recall Calvin ever admitting wrong, apologizing, or taking responsibility for failure. Calvin divided the world into the elect and the reprobate, the pious and the impious—and he was always on the right side while his enemies were always on the wrong side.

Unlike Calvin, Luther had a tormented conscience; he felt he could never do anything *right*, and it was this profound guilt that drove him to concoct his new theology. Luther was so convinced of his ineradicable corruption, guilt, and sinfulness that he despaired even of God's grace to change him. Even *to try* could lead only to frustration. The solution for Luther was not to focus on ethical behavior toward others but on absolving one's own conscience.

It really is an extraordinary position. "Whoever wants to be saved," Luther said, "should act as though no other human being except him existed on earth." In an important sense, the Reformation doctrine of grace flows from this one man's attempt to assuage his conscience. Luther articulated a brand-new theology, one that simply denied human freedom and insisted that man plays no role in his own salvation.

Now, to say that Luther and Calvin were flawed men is not surprising or informative. We could say that about anyone. Far more important to me was what I learned about how their flaws worked their way into Protestant theology, and ultimately into my life. There were cracks in the foundation of my religious tradition and those cracks found their way into my heart.

* * *

What does all this have to do with my marriage? I was discovering that my Protestant theology did not provide an adequate moral compass, sense of hope, or spiritual inspiration to meet the challenges of marriage. My historical studies further shook the foundations of my worldview, challenged me to deeper self-examination, and forced me to explore new answers to my moral malaise.

I became convinced that Reformation theology advanced neither Luther nor Calvin, as human beings, toward holiness. I began to see their theology, rather, as a highly sophisticated form of self-justification. In one sense this was an easy conclusion to reach, since I found in Luther and Calvin the very same flaws I found in myself. Therefore, if I was going to advance out of my morass, I was going to need different guides. Eventually, these concerns pushed me to seek holiness in the Catholic tradition and in the Catholic sacrament of marriage.

The intellectual history of Protestantism became for me a mirror in which to contemplate my own moral and spiritual dilemma. My tradition formed me to expect absolute assurance about salvation, regardless of my own behavior. Revealed in the lives of my Protestant mentors, though, I began to see how this attitude could have harmful effects not only on marriage, but on all manner of social relations.

I came to believe that my mentors and heroes in the faith had been worse than socially awkward: They had been dangerous ideologues, immune to criticism, utterly cocksure, and willing to impose their views with deadly force. This discovery was disquieting, to say the least. I always thought Catholics were the tyrants and ideologues, leading crusades and inquisitions and so forth, but now I was seeing the seed of interpersonal tyranny in *my own* tradition.

* * *

"One door, and only one, and yet its sides are two; I'm on the inside, on which side are you?"

Martin Luther was particularly given to this kind of thinking: "One side must be the Devil and God's enemy," he once wrote. "There is no middle ground." John Calvin similarly divided the world into the "pious" and the "impious," and he was utterly convinced of which side he was on. The "impious," he wrote to King Edward of England, should be repressed with the sword.

The Puritans of New England attempted to build an entire civilization on the distinction between the elect and the reprobate. Around the same time, the Westminster Confession of Faith (1647), which was composed in England to provide an authoritative guide for building such a Protestant civilization, promised that the elect can have an "infallible assurance" of their election.

In Protestant thinking, "elect and reprobate" is not the same thing as "good and bad." Instead, it is having "true faith" that distinguishes the elect from the reprobate. The elect, by virtue of having accepted that faith, can be *infallibly certain* that they are elect, even when their lives are morally disordered in other ways. Put crudely, you can meet an arrogant, self-righteous, lecherous egotist who *knows for sure* that he is one of God's elect, destined for Heaven.

I was that egotist.

Chapter 5

Rethinking Sex and Marriage

"Jill, would you go with me to a class on Natural Family Planning?"

Early 2000 was the low point in my marriage. Jill and I had almost quit talking. We had given up praying together, and our relationship had degraded to a series of hostile negotiations. We competed and fought over our priorities for time, space, and money. We were not even united enough to talk about marriage counseling, so it was absurd to think we might collaborate on something as life changing as Natural Family Planning.

NFP is a form of family planning that requires abstaining from sexual relations during the fertile periods of a woman's cycle if the couple decide to postpone childbearing. It is not easy and requires close cooperation and regular sacrifice.

What was I thinking?

While our marriage was deteriorating, however, my studies were forcing me more into questions of morality and Christian spirituality. I could not really talk to Jill about what I was learning, but I was slowly getting a broader perspective, especially about differences between Catholic and Protestant conceptions of marriage.

The Catholic ideal of married life is rigorous and difficult. Catholic spouses are to surrender their own selfish interests in service to a transcendent goal—to bring one's spouse and one's children to God. Sometimes that self-surrender calls for enormous and painful sacrifice, just as Jesus sacrificed Himself on the Cross for the sake of the Church. Most importantly, the Catholic Church recognizes Christian marriage as a sacrament, which means that God promises us the grace to meet those difficult demands.

Early Protestants, on the other hand, simply denied that marriage is a sacrament. Instead, they threw up their hands and asserted that the demands of Catholic marriage were too difficult. Therefore, they called for a relaxation of those demands and an end to the Church's control over marriage. Protestant thought went on to emphasize more strongly the sexual dimension of married life, and eventually the romantic element as well, while deemphasizing the role that suffering plays in union with God.

My Protestantism offered me little solace in the face of a hopeless marriage, but Catholicism seemed to offer me a way to reconceive my suffering. Suffering willingly embraced becomes sacrifice, and sacrifice can bring a deeper experience of God's grace.

But Natural Family Planning *requires* sacrifice, cooperation, and virtue: That is, it *requires* grace. We lacked all those things, but could we seek them out? Could we begin to reconceive our marital life on new terms? It was just the germ of an idea.

* * *

Iowa City is a small university town. Most of our life fell within a few square miles of modest homes and city parks. Birmingham, where we returned in the spring of 1999, is no metropolis, but it still offers a different pace of life. While we could walk most places we needed to go in Iowa, in Alabama everything required a car. Our plan was to expand Jill's social opportunities by moving south, but it backfired.

The problem of Jill's loneliness was compounded. In Iowa, Jill was buried in a tiny cave under a mountain of snow, like a momma polar bear hibernating with her cubs for the winter. It was lonely, but what else was there to do? In Birmingham, the world went zipping past, but there was no invitation to join the race. Meanwhile, I knew my life was on a clock: I needed to write like mad to finish my dissertation.

But the biggest change was children. We left Birmingham years ago, childless and idealistic. We returned jaded and with three small kids. Jill's overriding concern was their health: They may not have been much sicker than most small children, but with little else to do, Jill zeroed in on every potential threat.

Prince wrote a song in the 1980s called "1999," the chorus to which is "Tonight we're gonna party like it's 1999." I listened to that song in my teenage years wondering, "Where will I be on December 31, 1999?"

Well, two of my children—my four-year old son and eight-month old daughter—caught pneumonia in December that year. Their condition worsened and refused to respond to antibiotics. I remember my oldest, Jonathan, lying listless on the bed burning with fever. Finally, both were admitted to the hospital, where they were administered intravenous antibiotics. Jonathan needed a thoracentesis, in which a large needle is inserted into the abdomen to remove fluid from the lungs. My middle child, two-year-old Joshua, stayed home with a babysitter, terrified because his siblings had been taken away.

Jill and I sat up that night cradling our children at the hospital. Jill was distraught, nearly in tears, terrified that she might lose her oldest son. Zoey was crying in a hospital crib, an IV needle protruding from her head. I looked at the clock and noticed that it was about to strike midnight on 1999.

That night in the hospital was a low point of my life. My faith was ebbing away, and my wife was a nervous wreck. Graduate study dragged on and on, and we had barely enough money to live on.

And even as the finish line for my dissertation was coming into sight, the reality of the academic job market started weighing on my mind. Academic posts in the humanities are few, far between, and initially poorly paid. Old friends with far less education were moving along (and away from us) in business and in life. My little children were suffering in my arms. What did I want for them? How could I help them? Who could I be for them? My sense of myself and of the world was spinning out of control.

* * *

I spent most of my time that year studying and writing in the library at Samford University, a Baptist school with an interdenominational divinity school and an outstanding theological library. My interest in Catholicism was growing. I did not yet have any conscious plans to become Catholic; rather, I began by developing an intellectual fascination with an august tradition that boasted an unparalleled body of moral and spiritual reflection. On my breaks, I would often pull Catholic volumes off the shelves or read the *Catholic Encyclopedia*. Sometimes these sources would touch on marriage and sexuality.

My dissertation research also brought me into closer contact with the Catholic tradition. My work addressed Calvin's critique of late medieval spirituality. Among other things, Calvin rejected Catholic attitudes on sex, marriage, celibacy, and continence, and so I learned more about the Catholic tradition as I studied Calvin's rejection of it.

For the first time, I started thinking about the differences between Protestant and Catholic notions of sex and marriage. I discerned four major differences between the two traditions:

1. The Catholic tradition opposes both contraception and sodomy in marriage. Most Protestants allow them.
2. The Catholic Church exalts virginity, celibacy, and perfect continence over marriage. The Protestant tradition has always rejected this.

3. The Catholic Church does not allow Christian divorce and remarriage. Although Protestantism values lifelong fidelity in a broad sense, Protestant tradition has always allowed divorce in at least a few circumstances, such as adultery.
4. The Catholic Church regards Christian marriage as a *sacrament* that conveys grace. As a sacrament, Christian marriage (not all marriage) ought to be governed by Church law. Protestant tradition, rather, has always asserted that God ordains marriage, but not as a sacrament. For Protestants, marriage is a civil institution rightly governed by civil law.

Protestants and Catholics have different views of marriage, I came to understand, because they have different views about the foundational concepts of morality, spirituality, salvation, and human happiness. Catholics believe that the ultimate end of human life is loving union with God and neighbor. Aided by grace, we ought to bend every fiber of our being toward that end. Catholic ideas about marriage and contemplative life reflect that lofty calling.

The Protestant tradition also extols loving union with God but has always been more skeptical about the Christian's moral potential. Catholics take quite seriously Christ's command to "be perfect, as your heavenly Father is perfect" (Matt. 5:48). Relying on God's grace through prayer and the sacraments, and through diligent cooperation with grace, Catholics believe that all God's commands can be obeyed. By contrast, the Protestant tradition teaches that sin always remains and that perfect holiness in this life is impossible. Early Protestants argued, therefore, that we ought to relax the discipline of Christian life (including marriage) to accommodate human weakness.

I explored these questions piecemeal and accidentally while browsing the stacks at Samford University. The timing was, perhaps, providential: Crisis in my personal life and crisis in my theology made me more open to new ideas. I was not yet looking to become Catholic, but my admiration was growing. What moved me most in those early explorations was the Catholic regard for the dignity of the human person. The Catholic Church sees the human person not as a quivering bundle of corrupt sexual impulses but as a transcendent moral agent called to divine life. Surprisingly, it ended up being a Mormon, not a Catholic, who first opened my eyes to the Catholic theology of sex and marriage.

* * *

I happened one day on the ecumenical journal *First Things*, which offers commentary on social issues from a variety of religious perspectives, usually grounded in tradition and orthodoxy. Catholics, Protestants, Jews, Mormons, and, in at least one instance, Buddhists write social criticism from within their own traditions but aiming to address a wider audience.

A 1999 article by a Mormon physician, Joseph B. Stanford, M.D., initiated another step in my consideration of Catholicism. Dr. Stanford wrote about his discovery in medical school that hormonal contraception often causes the miscarriage of fertilized embryos. Learning this, Dr. Stanford determined never to prescribe "the pill."

Prompted by his discoveries about the Pill, he took up the subject of intentional sterilization. He realized that sterilization procedures do not cure any disease but merely damage healthy organs, preventing their proper function. Is this the purpose of medicine?

Through clinical practice, Dr. Stanford later became convinced that contraception in any form has a corrosive effect on marriage. Even if couples don't reflect consciously on it, contraception undeniably alters the meaning of marital sexuality. Dr. Stanford became convinced that contraception of any kind is contrary to the authentic meaning of marital life, and then offered a rigorous defense of NFP.

Stanford is not a Catholic, but a Mormon, and he acknowledged that his own tradition is largely silent on the question of contraception. Stanford's discoveries were not motivated by obedience to religious texts or other authorities, but by his study of pharmacology, clinical experience, and philosophical reflection on his practice of family medicine.

At the time I read the article, I knew about Catholic opposition to birth control. I had also met a few conservative Protestants who opposed the practice with scriptural arguments, but I found them unconvincing. I had never met someone who had reasoned his way into this position from scientific and philosophical arguments only. Again, it was Stanford's Mormonism that stood out to me. Had a Catholic written the same article, I don't think I would have taken it as seriously.

Emboldened, I took up Catholic reflection on contraception with a more open mind. As I studied, many old prejudices fell away. No, Catholics don't think you should have as many babies as you possibly can. No, the pope is not simply trying to grow the Church through fertility. And, no, Catholic opposition to birth control does not mean the Church is heedless of teen pregnancy, sexually transmitted diseases, or other dangers associated with sexual activity. Rather, I found that Catholics have developed a rich theology of the human person that takes full account of man's social, sexual, and psychological nature.

Moral theology, I came to understand, is more than just listing all the prohibitions mentioned in Scripture; it is the science of human happiness. Just as a physician prescribes treatments for the flourishing of the body, the moral theologian seeks the flourishing of the whole person by asking, "How can man act in the world to achieve his true good?"

Catholic reflection on birth control turns that question to the most intimate sphere: "How should a man act sexually to achieve real happiness?" My Protestant upbringing said simply that we are to limit sexual activity to marriage, but that within marriage we can do whatever pleases us. The modern secular attitude merely extends the emphasis on pleasure to all consensual activity, regardless of marital status. The Catholic Church, on the other hand, asks the faithful and the whole world to pursue the *true meaning* of sexual intimacy—a meaning that transcends the self. Sex is life-giving and life-affirming.

Intrigued, I looked more deeply into this strange Catholic doctrine by picking up Pope Paul VI's famous encyclical on the connection between human sexuality and human life, *Humanae Vitae*. I found that the pope's letter, contrary to stereotypes, was not a list of arbitrary or unreasonable prohibitions, but a beautiful description of the beauty and importance of marital friendship.

Biologists look at humans as a species of animal. Economists see units of production and consumption. But Catholics look at humans as persons: free, intelligent subjects capable of knowing and loving.

As persons, our greatest potential is for spiritual friendship, when we unite ourselves lovingly with others in pursuit of some noble good. For Pope Paul VI, marriage offers an opportunity for a particularly sublime form of spiritual friendship. Man and wife join indissolubly for the task of raising a family, and the loves and pleasures of married life take their proper form from that end. Paul VI says:

> It is a love which is total—that very special form of personal friendship in which husband and wife generously share everything, allowing no unreasonable exceptions and not thinking solely of their own convenience. Whoever really

> loves his partner loves not only for what he receives, but loves that partner for the partner's own sake, content to be able to enrich the other with the gift of himself.[6]

If you approach married life in that way, it becomes impossible to objectify your spouse for your own gratification. Instead, you beg for God's grace and bend every fiber to order your life toward this transcendent goal. You would be willing to bear suffering, abstinence, and abnegation if they serve that great good. You would, in fact, learn to imitate Christ.

* * *

"Would you come with me to a class on Natural Family Planning?"

"No way!" Jill replied. "Absolutely not. Why on earth would you want to do something like that?"

Jill and I had begun to lead very different parallel lives. We lived under the same roof, ate the same food, paid the same bills, and cared for our children, but our understanding of the meaning of our shared life had slowly and persistently drifted apart.

Jill's spiritual life had lost almost all its fervor amid the day-to-day concerns of raising three small children. She was isolated and felt deeply the loss of her sense of Christian vocation. I was suffering, too, but for different reasons. I was confused in my theology and in my life. I had moved to Birmingham to help my wife, but this now looked like a terrible idea, as her anxiety and depression had only deepened.

As I reexamined everything, I began to think that a life of academic research and teaching simply would not work for my family. How could I embark on the tenure treadmill when my family was hurting? Academic jobs, after all, are very unstable for everyone but the tenured elite.

[6] Paul VI, encyclical letter *Humanae Vitae* (July 25, 1968), no. 9.

My academic research felt increasingly disconnected from the concerns of daily life. What did sixteenth-century Geneva have to do with picking up antibiotics from the store for my kids? I didn't know how to articulate it, but I had a vague sense that our intimate life could be reformed, that somewhere in this mystery there was a key to a new life. I was desperate to find some way to reach out to my wife, to rekindle the sense of mission we once shared—and NFP was what I seized upon.

Jill was unimpressed.

"I won't go," she said. "You can go yourself, if you want."

And so I went.

I found a local chapter of the Couple to Couple League, which is an officially nonsectarian organization dedicated to teaching the principles of NFP. I found that in practice, though, it was heavily Roman Catholic. I turned out to be the only Protestant in the class.

"Why are you taking a course on NFP?" the instructors asked.

Most people in the class were simply trying to be faithful to Church teaching.

"I want to strengthen my marriage," I said.

And I meant it.

I tried to bring what I learned home to Jill, but unsurprisingly my life became more, not less, complicated.

Today, I appreciate that NFP is more than just a system for regulating fertility. It is a complete lifestyle that must be sustained by a shared philosophy, and it requires the virtues of selflessness, temperance, and charity. For Catholics, the spiritual life is dedicated to cultivating those virtues with the help of the sacraments. Without the sacraments and without the virtues, NFP is much more difficult—and perhaps impossible.

I would later learn that Catholic teaching acknowledges this difficulty. John Paul II taught that most people advance only gradually, in fits and starts, toward the integration of their moral and spiritual lives. The Church's job is not simply to impose a law on people, but to educate them, to offer grace to them, and to accompany them on the way. Without that grace and accompaniment, we weren't prepared to live this lifestyle in true faith, hope, and charity. But we were, I can now see, moving in the right direction.

* * *

Around this time I also began to study the ancient discipline of celibacy. But isn't celibacy a denial of the good of marriage, you might ask? That's what I used to think—that priests, monks, and nuns were just punishing themselves irrationally to "earn" Heaven. I learned instead what the *Catechism of the Catholic Church* teaches: "Esteem of virginity for the sake of the kingdom and the Christian understanding of marriage are inseparable, and they reinforce each other" (1620).

I spent much of my time in the library that year reading deeply in the history of Christian spirituality. Now, spirituality is not the same thing as religious doctrine. Whereas doctrine is about what Christian's believe, spirituality is about how we live that out—the practices and attitudes we cultivate to unite ourselves to God. As I studied, I started to see how celibacy and marriage could enrich one another.

No one can take up the study of ancient Christian spirituality today without feeling a bit disoriented. Many early Christians went to shocking lengths in pursuit of holiness, such as St. Symeon the Stylite (390–459) who spent thirty-seven years in seclusion atop a pillar in Syria. When I was a child, spirituality meant personal Bible study, petitionary prayer, youth groups, summer camps, and evangelistic appeals. It was something comfortable and familiar. For the ancients, however, spirituality was a radical call to transcend the limits of mere nature and to share in a supernatural life.

The theologians of the second through fourth centuries stressed that Christianity is a participation in the divine nature —an escape from sin, corruption, and ultimately from death. Christian martyrs and ascetics exemplified this ideal by their heroic lives of abnegation, and famous hermits, such as St. Antony of Egypt (251–356), fled to the desert, like Christ during His temptations. They battled their own bodies and minds in the quest for purity of heart. Their victories "proved" what was possible with grace.

These Christian ascetics were motivated not by hatred of the body or by a craven fear of damnation but by the promise of friendship with God. We can see this in the way St. Augustine, one of the great theologians of celibacy, wrote about sexual renunciation. As a young man, Augustine was filled with lust and worldly ambition. He worked as a professor of rhetoric, teaching the skills necessary for advancement in the culture of imperial Rome. He also kept a mistress to gratify his carnal desires.

Augustine felt unsatisfied with his life and trapped by his cravings. One day, a friend named Ponticianus told him the story of St. Antony. He recounted how the man had sold his possessions, given the proceeds to the poor, and fled to the desert to pursue God in prayer. Ponticianus explained how some of his own friends had also learned of St. Antony and given up their ambitions at court to become friends of God. In his *Confessions*, St. Augustine recounts his friend's story:

> What do we hope to gain by all the efforts we make? What are we looking for? What is our purpose in serving the state? Can we hope for anything better at court than to be the Emperor's friends? Even so, surely our position would be precarious and exposed to much danger. We shall meet it at every turn, only to meet another danger which is greater

> still. How long is it to be before we reach it? But if I wish, I can become the friend of God at this very moment.[7]

Augustine was inspired. He had felt trapped in his sins, but here was a man who was single-minded in his pursuit of God, and it showed him a better way to live. Augustine explained his frustration:

> What is the matter with us? What is the meaning of this story? These men have not had our schooling, yet they stand up and storm the gates of heaven, while we for all our learning lie here groveling in this world of flesh and blood.[8]

This was a theme Augustine returned to repeatedly throughout his life. Great philosophers through history have tried to explain sublime truths about the eternal world. They could praise great virtues, but they were powerless on their own to create those virtues in themselves or in others. In the Catholic Church, however, relatively simple men and women rose to the heights of sanctity.

Augustine did not despise marriage; indeed, he wrote one of the great Catholic treatises praising marriage, called, fittingly, *On the Good of Marriage*. What Augustine, Antony, and other ancient Christians valued most, though, was the idea of a life given wholly to God. Marriage is a good state of life, but Christian contemplation is better.

When I started reading about this ancient spirituality, I was surprised by how widespread it was. From Ireland to Persia, ancient Christians were almost unanimous in their praise of virginity and

[7] Augustine, *Confessions*, trans. R. S. Pine-Coffin (London: Penguin, 1961), 167–168.

[8] Ibid., 170.

continence.[9] Whatever else might be true about them, the earliest believers surely did not share modern Protestant attitudes toward sex.

This forced me to look at what the Bible says on these topics through a new lens. I had learned growing up that Catholic celibacy was not just unnatural but unbiblical. Augustine and Antony might agree that celibacy is "unnatural" in a certain sense, since we cannot live this way generously without supernatural grace. But the Church Fathers would never agree that this state of life is unbiblical. Gradually, I came to see that they were correct.

Christ Himself was unmarried, poor, and completely obedient to God. "Foxes have dens," Jesus said, "and birds of the air have nests; but the Son of Man has no place to lay his head" (Luke 9:58). "I have come ... not to do my own will, but the will of him who sent me" (John 6:38). "If any one comes to me and does not hate his own father and mother and wife and children and brothers and sisters, yes, and even his own life, he cannot be my disciple" (Luke 14:26).

Jesus acknowledged that not everyone is cut out for the kind of total abandonment implied by celibacy, but those who can should embrace it:

> Not all men can receive this precept, but only those to whom it is given. For there are eunuchs who have been so from birth, and there are eunuchs who have been made eunuchs by men, and there are eunuchs who have made themselves eunuchs for the sake of the kingdom of heaven. He who is able to receive this, let him receive it (Matt. 19:11–12).

[9] Peter Brown, *The Body and Society: Men, Women, and Sexual Renunciation in Early Christianity* (New York: Columbia University Press, 2008), 428–429.

St. Paul also counseled virginity. He urged young women not to marry, divorced women to remain single, and widows not to remarry. Not everyone has the gift to be able to pursue such a life, he acknowledged, but it is better to follow this way if possible. "He who marries his betrothed does well," Paul wrote, "and he who refrains from marriage will do better" (1 Cor. 7:38).

Scripture and history forced me to confront an important truth. The Catholic ideal of virginity and perfect continence was perfectly biblical. Jesus taught it and the ancient Church embraced it. The desert fathers and great ascetics lived it. Great theologians such as St. Augustine saw this message as liberating and positive, not as something hateful and oppressive. It was not abnegation for the sake of abnegation. It was abnegation for the sake of friendship with God.

* * *

The Catholic Church teaches that celibacy and marriage enrich one another, but how is this possible? The ideal of celibacy reminds all Christians that the goal of life is spiritual friendship, not personal aggrandizement or pleasure seeking. A few Christians can take up that life in radical detachment from the world, but many more Christians live spiritual friendship through marriage.

The Christian ideal of marriage was very different from the ancient Roman practice. Pagan society expected chastity of women, but not of men. Roman men were allowed prostitutes and concubines, and then to avoid the unwanted consequences of such promiscuity they resorted to forced abortions, infanticide, and rudimentary and extremely harmful contraceptives. Women suffered disproportionately from these practices, which became one of the reasons Roman women were more likely than men to become Christian. The Catholic doctrine on chastity was liberating.

The Catholic Church advocated personal commitment to God over all other social commitments, even for women. This was a particularly radical idea in patriarchal Rome, where women were expected as a matter of course to acquiesce to the will of men. The Church, however, venerated virgin martyrs, such as St. Lucy, who went to their deaths for refusing to marry against their will. Unlike many other cultures of the era, canon law has refused from the very beginning to recognize the validity of forced marriage.

The idea of celibacy, therefore, enriched Christian marriage by exalting the notions of freedom, holiness, and spiritual friendship. The result was a view of marriage with a real *purpose* that went well beyond sexual satisfaction: growing in holiness *together*. The ancient writer Tertullian, following the teaching of St. Paul, advised his wife not to remarry if he were to die. He also penned one of the most touching descriptions of Christian marriage:

> How beautiful, then, the marriage of two Christians, two who are one in hope, one in desire, one in the way of life they follow, one in the religion they practice. They are as brother and sister, both servants of the same Master. Nothing divides them, either in flesh or in spirit. They are, in very truth, two in one flesh; and where there is but one flesh there is also but one spirit. They pray together, they worship together, they fast together; instructing one another, encouraging one another, strengthening one another. Side by side they visit God's church and partake of God's Banquet; side by side they face difficulties and persecution, share their consolations. They have no secrets from one another; they never shun each other's company; they never bring sorrow to each other's hearts. Unembarrassed they visit the sick and assist the needy. They give alms without anxiety; they attend the Sacrifice without difficulty; they perform their

> daily exercises of piety without hindrance. They need not be furtive about making the Sign of the Cross, nor timorous in greeting the brethren, nor silent in asking a blessing of God. Psalms and hymns they sing to one another, striving to see which one of them will chant more beautifully the praises of their Lord. Hearing and seeing this, Christ rejoices. To such as these He gives His peace. Where there are two together, there also He is present; and where He is, there evil is not.[10]

As I studied the lives of these ancient Christian writers, I found something very different from the spirituality of my youth—something inspiring and hopeful. Catholicism taught that with the help of grace, we can escape our narrow self-absorption and give ourselves to something truly noble and beautiful. Catholics did not despise sex and marriage: They subordinated them to something transcendent.

* * *

As my own marriage was falling apart, I was attracted to this ideal of spiritual friendship. Would it really be possible to reform our marriage according to this idea, and then to appeal to God for the grace to live it? The example of ancient Christians suggested that anything could be possible with God (see Luke 1:37).

My historical studies then led me to ask why early Protestants reacted so vehemently against Catholic ideas about marriage and celibacy. At root, early Protestant theologians thought the Catholic position was simply too difficult. Many people fail to achieve the ideal of Catholic marriage, and sometimes their failures are positively scandalous. In the sixteenth-century, Protestant writers

[10]Tertullian, "To His Wife," in *Treatises on Marriage and Remarriage*, *Ancient Christian Writers Series*, no. 13, trans. William P. LeSaint, S.J. (Westminster, MD: Newman Press, 1951), 35–36.

responded to these scandals by calling for a relaxation of Church law. The Lutheran Augsburg Confession (1530) made this point explicitly: "Man's nature is gradually growing weaker," it said, and "the old rigor ought ... to be relaxed because of the weakness of men" (XXIII.14–15).

Earlier, Martin Luther himself rejected the Catholic doctrine of marriage and celibacy because he thought it was impossible. In 1522, he preached a sermon on marriage called "Increase and Multiply." His advice is shocking even to Protestants today: "As little as we can do without eating and drinking," he preached, "just as impossible is it to abstain from women.... He who resolves to remain single let him give up the name of human being.... If the wife refuses, let the servant maid come."[11]

Luther made further surprising concessions to sexual weakness. He argued that a woman married to an impotent man ought to be allowed intercourse with another, perhaps the man's brother: "The woman is free through divine law and cannot be compelled to suppress her carnal desires." With some reservation, Luther also approved the bigamous marriage of Philip of Hesse.[12]

The Reformers discussed marriage and celibacy at length, but they rarely discussed contraception or marital sodomy. When they did, however, they affirmed the traditional Catholic prohibition on these practices, and, in fact, until the twentieth century most Protestants retained the Catholic teaching on these issues.[13] Eventually, however, the logic of Luther's doctrine worked its way through

[11] James Reston, *Luther's Fortress: Martin Luther and His Reformation under Siege* (NY: Basic Books, 2015), 222–223.

[12] Ibid., 90–91.

[13] John Tuskey, "The Elephant in the Room—Contraception and the Renaissance of Traditional Marriage," *Regent University Law Review* 18, no. 2 (Spring 2006): 315–325.

Protestantism, and today the presumption of Protestant preachers is in favor of sexual license.

* * *

The modern American sexual ethic, as far as I can tell, consists in two absolutes: First, consent legitimizes any sexual activity, and second, it is wrong to suppress sexual desire unless that desire is directed toward those who cannot give consent. These are the values we see championed in contemporary law, entertainment, and psychology.

Protestant sexual ethics, as I experienced it growing up, basically accepts those two points with only one important qualification: marriage. For evangelical Protestants, consent legitimizes *married* sexual activity, and it is wrong to suppress sexual desire if it can be sublimated or gratified through *married* sexual activity.

The Protestants I grew up with were keen to dispel any notion that they disparaged sex. In college, I heard lectures that praised the Puritans for *compelling* married sexual activity. I learned that husbands and wives have a *duty* to gratify one another. I never heard a sermon, message, catechetical lecture, or private counsel that ever suggested moderating or taming sexual desire or activity within marriage.

The Protestant ministry Focus on the Family is representative of mainstream evangelical thinking on sex and marriage. Psychologist James Dobson founded the organization in 1977, and today it has an operating budget of almost $100 million that it uses to promote a Protestant and conservative vision of family life through counseling, book publishing, radio broadcasts, and other media. Pastors and leaders that I have known frequently cite Dobson and his ministry as authorities on marriage, family, and sexuality. The organization was even inducted into the Radio Hall of Fame in 2008 for its influential work in media.

Focus on the Family's website today includes articles with titles such as "Red-Hot Monogamy: Making Your Marriage Sizzle," "No More Headaches: Enjoying Sex and Intimacy in Marriage," and "The Five Sex Needs of Men and Women: Discover the Secrets of Great Sex in a Godly Marriage." A website article on oral sex explains what I have found to be typical of modern, Protestant sexual ethics:

> God has entrusted solely to a husband and wife the prerogative of defining the particulars of their sexual relationship. No one else has the right or authority to tell them how to behave in the bedroom provided it does not violate Scripture.... To put it another way, mutual consent is basic to all healthy sexual expression in marriage.[14]

A few years ago, evangelical megachurch pastor Mark Driscoll gained notoriety by preaching sexually explicit sermons in which he counseled husbands and wives to engage in various forms of noncoital sexual activity and publicly urged wives to do their duty by performing oral sex on their husbands. His explicit language struck many people as pornographic. Protestant leaders at the time denounced Driscoll for going too far, but Driscoll's position did not surprise me. His style was explicit, but his basic message was consistent with what I always heard from Protestant leaders.

* * *

The differences between Protestant and Catholic teaching on marriage have their roots in two fundamental issues. First, the Protestant Reformers thought that Catholic teaching on human

[14]"Oral Sex as Appropriate Sexual Expression in Marriage," Focus on the Family, https://www.focusonthefamily.com/family-q-and-a/relationships-and-marriage/oral-sex-as-appropriate-sexual-expression-in-marriage.

sexuality was just too difficult. Second, the Reformers resented the authority that the Catholic Church exercised over Christian marriage. The way they tried to solve these "problems" theologically was to naturalize Christian marriage, removing it from the realm of the supernatural. A major part of the Reformation, therefore, was an attack on the sacramentality of Christian marriage.

The Reformers never denied that God instituted marriage at the creation of Adam and Eve. They simply denied that Christ elevated marriage to a sacrament. "Marriage is a good and holy ordinance of God," Calvin wrote, "and farming, building, cobbling, and barbering are lawful ordinances of God, and yet are not sacraments."[15] You could not ask for better proof that the Reformers wanted to naturalize marriage.

The Catholic Church acknowledges that there is such a thing as a purely natural marriage, which God instituted at creation. Such a marriage is a covenant "by which a man and a woman establish between themselves a partnership of the whole of life, [which] is by its nature ordered toward the good of the spouses and the procreation and education of offspring" (CCC 1601).[16]

This is the kind of marriage that existed everywhere before the coming of Christ. Natural marriages continue to exist today whenever at least one of the parties is unbaptized. You do not have to be a Catholic, a Christian, or even a religious believer to recognize this kind of marriage or to experience it, because it is rooted in our humanity as male and female, and thus proceeds from natural law.

But what about the sacrament of marriage? According to the Catholic Church, Christ elevated Christian marriage to a sacrament. In fact, "a valid matrimonial contract cannot exist between

[15]*Institutes of the Christian Religion*, 4.19.34.

[16]Quoting *Code of Canon Law*, 1055.1.

the baptized without it being by that fact a sacrament."[17] Was there any evidence for this idea in Scripture? As I thought about this, I realized four things about the scriptural teaching on marriage that suggested that the Catholics were right.

The first and most obvious fact was that Christ established a clear distinction between marriage under the old law and marriage restored by Christ. When the Pharisees questioned Jesus about divorce in the Mosaic Law, he acknowledged that Moses allowed this because of their "hardness of heart" (Matt. 19:8). But now, Christ was calling His disciples to the perfection of marriage only possible by grace.

Second, I realized that Scripture continued to affirm a difference between Christian marriage and non-Christian marriage. In his First Letter to the Corinthians, St. Paul holds the marriage of two baptized Christians to a higher standard than that of a Christian to a non-Christian. The so-called "Pauline privilege" allows for the dissolution of a marriage between two unbelievers if one of them becomes a Christian and the non-Christian party is unwilling to remain in the marriage (1 Cor. 7:17–20). Between Christians, however, Paul allows no dissolution of the bond (1 Cor. 7:11).

The third realization was the most shocking to me, but perhaps the most significant. In 1 Corinthians 6, St. Paul teaches that Christians must not engage in sexually immoral behavior. That is not terribly surprising. What is surprising is the reason he gives. "Do you not know that your bodies are members of Christ?" Paul writes, "Shall I therefore take the members of Christ and make them members of a prostitute? Never!" (1 Cor. 6:15).

In this text, Paul teaches that a Christian's very body has been permanently changed in a way that identifies him with Christ and thereby affects his sexuality. The Christian literally carries the body

[17]*Code of Canon Law*, 1055.2.

of Christ with him into the marriage bed. While I found the idea to be somewhat arresting, I quickly saw that it had profound implications for the doctrine of marriage. If *two* baptized people got married, then Christ would necessarily be implicated in a very profound, very intimate way in their union. There was no way I could continue to conceive of Christian marriage as a merely "natural" union.

Finally, I considered the major scriptural text on the sacramentality of Christian marriage. In the fifth chapter of Ephesians, St. Paul clearly teaches that Christian marriage is a sign or symbol of Christ's marriage to the Church. He writes:

> Husbands, love your wives, as Christ loved the church and gave himself up for her, that he might sanctify her, having cleansed her by the washing of water with the word, that he might present the church to himself in splendor, without spot or wrinkle or any such thing, that she might be holy and without blemish. Even so husbands should love their wives as their own bodies. He who loves his wife loves himself. For no man ever hates his own flesh, but nourishes and cherishes it, as Christ does the church, because we are members of his body. "For this reason a man shall leave his father and mother and be joined to his wife, and the two shall become one flesh." This is a great mystery, and I mean in reference to Christ and the church (Eph. 5:25–32)

St. Paul connects the holiness of Christian marriage to the mystery of Christ's Body, the Church. As holiness flows from Christ to the Church, so, in a way, holiness flows from the sanctified bodies of the baptized to their spouses, because of their union with Christ. The "husband is consecrated through his wife," Paul writes elsewhere, and the "wife is consecrated through her husband" (1 Cor. 7:14).

When I reflected on these biblical truths, I saw that the Catholic doctrine on the sacrament of marriage made good sense. The essence of a sacrament is that it is a sign or symbol, instituted by Christ, that, by the power of the Holy Spirit really effects the thing signified. Clearly, Scripture teaches that Christian marriage is a sign of Christ's marriage to the Church, and of the holiness flowing from that union. Moreover, Christ expects Christians to experience a holiness in marriage not possible under the old law, or outside of Christ. Finally, it is obvious that the holiness of Christian marriage flows from our union to Christ in baptism.

There is more to Catholic marriage than what can be clearly seen in Scripture. Sacred Tradition also informs the Catholic position on marriage and ties together the threads of scriptural teaching in a beautiful way. It takes more than "Scripture alone" to find perfect clarity and certainty in this doctrine. But my reflection on Scripture showed me that the Catholic position could not be lightly dismissed. Finally, the Catholic position offered something I desperately needed: the transformation of marriage from the realm of mere nature into something transcendently and supernaturally beautiful.

* * *

"Father, how do you manage to live a celibate life?"

Before I finally entered the Catholic Church in 2003, I made my first confession one Saturday afternoon in November. For most of my Protestant life, I viewed the confessional as a dark and mysterious, but also fascinating, place. The Catholic priesthood was also something bizarre and otherworldly. That Saturday afternoon, I opened my soul to a stranger—and I also took the opportunity to question him on something that always interested me.

"Chastity is hard, Father," I told him. "It's hard for me, and I'm married. But you are completely celibate and continent. How do you do it?"

I expected him to explain his daily regimen of self-denial—a discourse on prayers, penance, spiritual disciplines, and a grim determination to resist temptation. His response surprised me, but touched me deeply.

He smiled at me benevolently and answered immediately and without hesitation: "Relationship with God."

I have never forgotten that first confession. It was the perfect way to begin my Catholic life that reminded me that the ultimate purpose of Catholic life is a transcendent, empowering relationship with God.

The Catholic Church asks something of us that is naturally impossible. But "what is impossible with men is possible with God" (Luke 18:27).

Chapter 6

Thérèse and Prayer with the Saints

The first time I ever prayed to a saint, I worried God might strike me dead.

Catholics who have grown up with the saints can't appreciate the horror that many Protestants experience when witnessing Catholic devotion, which, to some, appears indistinguishable from pagan idolatry, including image worship, bacchanalian festivals, and rank superstition.

Studying Church history forced me to confront an uncomfortable truth: Devotion to the saints was everywhere in early Christianity. It was so ancient, so widespread, and so deeply embedded in the tradition that one could not draw a line between "Christian practice" and "veneration of saints" until the sixteenth century. I also discovered that the practice had roots not in pagan cultures but in Judaism and Scripture itself. In fact, such veneration *offended* pagans, who kept the remains of the dead strictly separate from public worship.

Virginity and martyrdom were the heroic ideals of early Christianity. Those who could not achieve martyrdom often fled to the deserts to pursue the consecrated life of Christian prayer. So many did this that St. Athanasius boasted, "The desert has become a city." But while many early Christians pursued this kind of heroic asceticism, many more remained at home, in family life and in earthly pursuits. They shared in the spirituality of Christian heroes not by imitating their asceticism but by venerating their bones, begging their prayers, and believing in the power of their intercession.

As my first year of research in Birmingham ended, I found the practice of praying to the saints to be abhorrent. The lives of the saints, however, attracted me. The ancient martyrs awed me with their fortitude. St. Antony the hermit astonished me with his self-denial. The life of St. Francis was more romantic than any Hollywood blockbuster.

I was by now willing to concede that Catholics, for all their superstition, had gotten at least some things right. They may even have had some insights Protestants needed. I was also interested in how the example of saints might be a positive influence on my marriage. It seemed reasonable, therefore, to explore this new country a bit more. I already read my way in to a lot of Catholic theology; now it was time to dig more deeply into the lives of the saints.

Sometime in the early 2000s, I discovered a saint who acted more immediately and more supernaturally on my soul and my marriage than any other—Thérèse of Lisieux. Thérèse inspired me with a spirituality I could apply directly to my marriage. She was also, eventually, the first saint to whom I ever addressed a prayer. Her prayers and intercessions, I believe, were directly related to my conversion to Catholicism, to my wife's newly awakening faith, and to the healing of my marriage.

* * *

I do not remember how I discovered Thérèse or why I became interested in her, but sometime around 2000 I took up the autobiography of this French Carmelite nun. Though I still considered myself a Calvinist at the time, what I found in Thérèse, even though she was a cloistered nun, was easily accessible to non-Catholics. She lived her faith with such generosity and simplicity, but also gritty realism, that it was impossible to dismiss her.

To say that Thérèse was accessible does not mean that she diminished the distinctly Catholic elements of her spirituality. On the contrary, it would be hard to find a more distinctly Roman Catholic life. Her parents were extremely devout Catholics (and are now canonized saints), and her sisters all became consecrated religious. Her life was consumed with the saints, the sacraments, the sacred priesthood, and devotion to the pope. Thérèse lived her spirituality not despite her Catholicism, but through it. She taught me that Catholic spirituality was not all about heroic flights to the desert, glorious martyrdom, consecrated virginity, or worshipping dead bones. She helped me see how the whole apparatus of Catholic life, for all its exotic flair, could be reduced to a very simple formula: "Have mercy on me, a sinner. O God, come to my aid."

Sometimes converts feel torn about leaving their childhood religion. Every tradition has something beautiful about it, and you can't take it all with you when you leave. One of the most attractive parts of evangelical Protestantism, for me, was the warmth and affective appeal of its spirituality. The sense of acceptance and childlike trust in God's love that is so much a part of that tradition is powerful and comforting. Protestant spirituality nourishes an awareness of God's forgiveness and a sense of intimacy with Him despite your own flaws and failures.

Protestant spirituality also encourages the active ministry of laypeople. Everyone is a priest, and therefore everyone is responsible for the mission of the Church. Protestants view daily life as a domain for active ministry. There are no separate sacred spaces: God must be served and worshipped everywhere. When I was Protestant, these things infused a sense of transcendence into daily life. They were also, we thought, things that separated us from Catholics.

Thérèse surprised me by exhibiting all these attitudes, and to a remarkable degree. She had a strong sense of lay priestly vocation and responsibility for the Church's mission. Her writing is filled with an awareness of predestination to grace, of divine providence and election, of the sanctification of daily life, and of personal relationship with Christ.

I once regarded these as almost uniquely Protestant attitudes. In my view, Catholics thought only the ordained priesthood had a vocation to ministry, and everyone else had to work out their salvation as if it all depended on their effort. Thérèse upended these stereotypes.

* * *

Thérèse Martin was born in 1873 in Alençon, France, to bourgeois Catholic parents. Her home life was almost idyllic. Thérèse's parents were loving, kind people of great faith, and everyone doted on Thérèse as the youngest of five sisters. If there was anything extreme about her early life, it would have been only how frilly, saccharine, and precious everything appears. In her autobiography, *The Story of a Soul*, Thérèse reminisces about flower petals, walks with her father, and games with her friends. Commentators remark on how small everything seems in Thérèse's world, and not a few readers have been turned off at first by her teeny, tiny world of girlish piety and social privilege.

Thérèse became a Carmelite nun at a young age. Was this perhaps a bit severe or excessive? Her decision makes more sense when we consider that she was following her older sisters into religious life and that both her parents had once nurtured hopes of entering the monastery. Eventually, every one of the Martin girls would become nuns. The most shocking thing about Thérèse's life might be that she became famous at all.

Why did this middle-class French girl become a paragon of spiritual strength known throughout the world? In her convent in Lisieux, the tiny saint made a profound impression on her religious sisters, so much so that her superior ordered her to write her memoirs in order to make her spirituality available to others. It is that record of her life that vaulted her to worldwide fame after her death at the age of twenty-four.

The Story of a Soul reveals a girl absolutely consumed with spiritual ambition—not an ambition to become famous, to excel in self-discipline, or even to write a world-class autobiography, but rather to identify with Christ and, in Him, to know the love of God. She set out not to do big things for God but simply to do everything for Him, no matter how small. "Miss no single opportunity of making some small sacrifice," she wrote, "here by a smiling look, there by a kindly word; always doing the smallest right and doing it all for love."[18]

Thérèse identified powerfully with the mission of the universal Church and with the Catholic priesthood. She understood her vocation to be saving souls and praying for priests, and she had a strong impulse for missionary work. Unable to travel, she made of her simple life an offering for the advancement of the gospel. "What I came to do at the Carmelites," she explained, "I declared ... at the foot of Jesus the Holy Host, at the examination which preceded my profession, 'I came to save souls, and above all to pray for priests.'"

These are noble sentiments, but they aren't terribly uncommon among Catholic nuns. What made Thérèse's spirituality unique?

[18] *Autobiography of a Saint*, trans. Ronald Knox (London: Collins, 1973), 187.

It might be helpful to contrast Thérèse, the "little Teresa," with the saint sometimes known as the "Big Teresa," Teresa of Avila.

The Spanish mystic of the sixteenth century was also a cloistered Carmelite nun who wrote her life story under obedience. But the Big Teresa aimed undeniably at big things: She became a religious superior who gave spiritual direction to others and ultimately a reformer who refashioned the Carmelite order. She was not immune to ecclesiastical politics, and she even once had to defend herself before the inquisition. Finally, the Big Teresa taught a spirituality that is admirable but not a little intimidating. Her raptures, ecstasies, and severe interior life are not the kind of thing an average person can identify with. Little Thérèse knew all about the Big Teresa, but she did not follow her. She decided instead to pursue what would be called her "little way."

Thérèse understood that her early life had been sheltered and privileged, and she regarded this as a kind of temptation. Sometimes young people respond to such a realization by actively rejecting their comfortable family life in a quest for authenticity, heading off to foreign lands or on grand ideological ventures. A few, like St. Francis, come to great sanctity by such efforts. But many more, I suspect, fall eventually into disillusionment.

Thérèse took a different route. She neither went off on adventures nor retreated into a world of self-assured, comfortable devotion. She understood fully that to follow Christ means to take up the way of the Cross and to embrace suffering. But how can you do that if you are not called to great endeavors in the world? Thérèse made it her goal to accept the smallest trials and difficulties of life with utter resignation to the will of God. It didn't matter how "little" the trial: Everything became an opportunity to identify with Christ.

As an example, Thérèse recounts the conflicts she had with her religious superior. Mother Mary Gonzaga was not particularly tender toward Thérèse and could even be downright demeaning.

The young nun explains how Gonzaga would insult her in front of the sisters by disparaging her work in the convent. But Thérèse found in this experience a path to sanctity. Here is her report:

> She always treated me like this. How I thank God, my darling Mother, for such a virile and valuable training. What a priceless grace! I do not know what would have happened to me if I had become pet of the Community, as those outside seemed to think! I would probably have thought of my Superiors merely as human beings, instead of seeing Our Lord in them, and the heart that had been so well guarded in the world would have fallen prey to human attachments in the cloister. Luckily, I escaped such a fate. I can honestly say that, from the moment I entered, suffering opened her arms to me, not only in the trials I have already told you about, but in others keener still; and I embraced her lovingly. I declared my reason for coming to Carmel during the solemn examination before Profession: "I have come to save souls and above all to pray for priests," and when one wants to attain some end, one must take the means. As Jesus had made me realize that the Cross was the means by which He would give me souls, the more often it came my way, the more suffering attracted me. For five years I followed this course, though I was the only one to know it, and this practice was nothing else but the hidden flower I wanted to offer to Jesus, the flower whose perfume none would breathe this side of Heaven.[19]

Eventually, Thérèse's resolution would be tested by genuinely horrible pain from the tuberculosis that eventually killed her. Worse yet, she was assaulted with wracking doubts about the goodness and

[19]*The Story of a Soul: The Autobiography of the Little Flower* (Charlotte, NC: TAN Books, 2010), 87.

even the existence of God. Through it all, she regarded her "dark night of the soul" as yet one more opportunity to "know the love of Christ which surpasses knowledge" (Eph. 3:19).

Thérèse expressed a powerful sense of election—of predestination to grace—that is very familiar to Calvinists. Her nickname, the Little Flower, illustrates this. In *The Story of a Soul*, Thérèse tells us she came to see the world as something like God's flower garden. I can't help but wince a bit at the preciousness of the image, but it expresses a beautiful truth.

In a garden, Thérèse explains, not every plant enjoys the same prestige: Some are big, and some are little; some give structure to the space, and some simply adorn the beauty of the whole. The proper way to regard the garden, though, is to view the whole thing. And the key to life, she concluded, was to regard one's life as planted by God exactly where He wanted it. She imagined her own role to be that of a very little flower chosen by God.

I became fascinated by Thérèse. My childhood was like hers in some respects: I also grew up in a warm and loving middle-class home of strong religious faith, and I regarded foreign missionaries with a kind of awe. Our church romanticized their work, and it seemed to me to be a very noble calling. However, it was a calling for which I felt inadequate. Like Thérèse, I realized that was not my path. But *unlike* Thérèse, I had not yet found a path to genuine holiness in daily life.

I had a profession, but I had not yet recognized my vocation to sanctity. I took up the study of theology thinking this was my spirituality and that research and teaching would be my service to the Church. Since only faith saves, the only thing that matters is teaching the faith. I did not yet realize how worthless this is without the Cross.

I was suffering deeply in my marriage, and I lacked the virtues needed for daily life. Maybe I would go to Heaven when I died,

I thought, but what on earth do I do *now*? By embracing the smallest sacrifices of daily life and uniting them to the sufferings of Christ and to the mission of the Church, Thérèse helped me to see more deeply the poverty of my spiritual life—but also a way forward.

My own spirituality lacked this depth. We can merit nothing from God, I thought, and so nothing we do can have any transcendent value. It is only what Christ does for us that matters. Christians might take up the work of preaching, teaching, and proselytism to advance the Church, and such work might call for suffering and sacrifice, like any noble calling, but that suffering and sacrifice *per se* could not make the work more spiritually efficacious, more valuable, or more pleasing to God. This was a recipe for despair.

Thérèse exhibited all the littleness, the humility, and the reliance upon God's grace that I associated with Protestant spirituality. She also had a powerful sense of mission, of priesthood, and of responsibility to advance the Church. But Thérèse united these things to the most mundane activities of daily life. And she did so in a distinctly Catholic idiom, with Catholic assumptions, Catholic ideas, Catholic practices, and Catholic aspirations. Because they were united to Christ and to the sacrifice of the Mass, her sufferings and sorrows in the smallest things could have great value to God: In ways known only to Him, they advanced the mission of the gospel and the work of the Church.

Thérèse began to fill in the gaps for me. I began to see how Catholic spirituality might work in the heart of a simple person to bring hope and holiness.

She brought the exotic appearance of Catholic life down to earth for me and she inspired me with a vision of the work and suffering of daily life that was more transcendently meaningful than any I had yet known.

* * *

The example of Thérèse inspired me, but I was not yet ready to pray to her or to any saint. But that didn't stop the Little Flower from praying *for me* during the darkest period of my life.

Around this time I took a job south of Birmingham, and Jill and I moved to a new neighborhood to be near work. We moved across the street from a devout Catholic woman named Ellen Marie Edmonds, who is today a respected Catholic author and speaker known for her work on the challenge of dementia. I knew her then only as that nice Catholic lady across the street.

Years later, I learned that Ellen began praying for us as soon as she met us. Specifically, she prayed to St. Thérèse of Lisieux, asking that she lead us to the Catholic Church. They were prayers that I desperately needed, since I was about to enter the most difficult period in my spiritual journey.

I can't be certain on this side of the veil that Thérèse responded to those prayers—but I have every reason to believe she did. She provided two powerful signs of her intercession, which I will describe in their proper place. Though I still did not have Catholic faith, the intercession of the saints was beginning to work in my life.

Chapter 7

I Could Become a Catholic

I wanted to salvage both my Protestant faith and my marriage. And in the spring of 2000, I thought I had found a way to do both.

Our first year in Birmingham brought neither healing nor security. After our children's spell with pneumonia, Jill retreated into her life of maternal protection. I was just as caught up in my studies, but still months away from finishing my dissertation, and the pressure was mounting: My fellowship was running out, and we needed money. Jill had no knowledge of my theological struggles, but she did understand our material plight. She resented what my education had cost us in time and opportunity.

Our oldest child, Jonathan, was approaching kindergarten, so we needed to make decisions about his education. At the doctor's office, Jill met a woman whose children attended a new "classical" school. Jill was intrigued, and I liked the sound of it, too. To me, "classical" meant Latin and Greek, immersion in the Great Books, and a heavy emphasis on writing, speaking, logic, and dialectic. It was the kind of education I wished that I had had. We decided to apply.

The school was a ministry of a local Presbyterian Church, which appealed to me as a way to double down on my Presbyterian heritage as my doubts expanded. I was strongly resisting the allure of Catholicism. I really, really didn't want to become a Catholic, and cultivating my Presbyterian tradition seemed like the best way to avoid that. I thought that in a "classical" and confessional Presbyterian school, I could gratify my interest in tradition while retaining a firm Protestant identity.

The school required parents to be interviewed for admission to ensure that everyone bought into the school's educational vision. When Jill and I arrived, they began asking us about our background, church practice, and belief.

After nearly ten years of theological study and a lifetime spent in Protestant churches, I knew my theology very well. I answered their questions with enthusiasm and with great attention to Presbyterian history. I also revealed that I was a seminary graduate, working toward a Ph.D. in historical theology with a focus on John Calvin. They must have liked what they heard, because not only did they admit our child to the school, but they also offered me a job.

"We are looking for a headmaster. Are you interested?"

I was astounded. A thousand swirling pieces seemed to come together in my mind. Here, potentially, was the solution to my problems. I could support my wife in an academic vocation without trudging down the lonely road of tenure. We would have a community of families ready-made to receive us. And, best of all, providence seemed to be pointing out the solution to my theological struggles. I could embrace the path of a confessional Protestant.

Jill was also spellbound. She didn't yet know about my theological struggles, but she knew very well that my professional future could prove unstable. Like me, she was attracted to the promise of stability, community, income, and a structured way to raise our children.

It took only a few days for us to decide. I called the board member who offered me the job to accept the position.

I took this job hoping to recast my life, my marriage, my community, and my theology. And that was exactly what happened—but not in the way I expected. I spent only a year at the school, but it marked a major turning point in my life. At the end of that year I realized for the first time that Catholicism was a genuine possibility. I could become a Catholic.

* * *

The Catholic Church invented classical education. It is ironic, therefore, that there was a lot of anti-Catholicism in the classical school movement. In our school, for instance, studying history meant indoctrinating students in the narrative of the Reformation. One of our textbooks even taught that the Catholic Church had apostatized at the Council of Trent.

You might think I would have recoiled at this anti-Catholicism, but in fact I embraced it. The truth is that I was still eager to reject Catholicism. The institutional Catholic Church was still abhorrent to me, even if I had begun to rethink some of my other anti-Catholic prejudices. At most, I was trying to integrate a few elements of the Catholic tradition into my Presbyterian faith. There were two times, though, that I did think the anti-Catholicism had gone too far.

When I was hired, I knew nothing about school administration, so the board sent me to classical-school training in Moscow, Idaho. Moscow was something like the Mecca, or perhaps the Vatican, of the classical-school movement. An Idaho pastor named Doug Wilson founded the Association of Classical Christian Schools and over time created an empire in conservative Presbyterian circles. He publishes books and magazines, founded a new denomination, and started a college.

I will never forget the conversation I had in Idaho with a board member from another classical school. Our talk turned to whether Roman Catholics should be admitted to classical schools.

"When we began," she told me, "we had a number of Roman Catholic families involved at the school. After a few years, the board decided to implement a stricter doctrinal statement. All the parents were required to sign it. The Catholics wouldn't sign."

"You kicked them out?" I asked.

"Well, they wouldn't sign," she said. "They decided that loyalty to an institution was more important than fidelity to Christ."

I was dumbfounded and more than a bit disgusted. I didn't mind that they wanted a strict doctrinal statement: If you want a Protestant school, you should be able to set up a Protestant school. What repulsed me, though, was the betrayal of their existing parents and student body. Parents had invested their time, money, and children in one vision, and then the board shifted radically in midstream. They invited Catholic families to participate and then threw them out.

What bothered me even more was how casually this woman dismissed the Catholics' grievance: "Oh, they chose an institution over Christ." This was a gross misrepresentation of Catholic faith. Even worse, this woman equated faith in Christ with submission to a policy instituted last week! I couldn't believe the hubris.

The second time I worried about anti-Catholic bias occurred in a discussion with my board about our own admissions policy. Prospective parents were asked to fill out a questionnaire on their beliefs. Two questions came directly from James Kennedy's manual on evangelization. They read:

- † If you died tonight, do you know for sure that you would go to Heaven?
- † If God asked why He should let you in, what would you say?

These questions were meant to test the parents' attachment to the doctrine of "faith alone." The "correct" answers were supposed to be: "I know for sure" and "Only because of the grace of Christ."

I knew that a Roman Catholic could answer the second question "correctly." However, Catholics do not claim absolute assurance of salvation. Since Christ told us we must persevere to be saved, no Catholic claims to know for sure that he is going to Heaven.

I argued strongly that we should drop the first question: "Do we really want to exclude people because they lack assurance?" I did not raise the theological question of whether Catholics could be saved. I focused more on the significance of religious psychology: Do we really want to equate Christianity with the subjective psychological state of assurance?

The board agreed. We dropped the first question.

* * *

My experience at the school only exacerbated the tension between my growing sympathy with Catholics as people and my distaste for the institutional Catholic Church. On the one hand, I was eager to retain my Protestant faith and to resist the allure of Catholicism. On the other hand, I was troubled that my fellow Protestants seemed to have such a narrow view of the Catholicism they were rejecting.

I also witnessed theological tensions in the school leadership. I slowly learned that there were two factions represented on the school's board: members of the sponsoring church and members from another local Presbyterian church. The members from the sponsoring church were more evangelical and pietistic, while the others were more traditional. They disagreed about what it means to be a Presbyterian and to offer a classical education. In the years after my departure, there was a clear victor in the conflict, and a purge of the losing faction.

The pietist group identified with a movement called "Sonship theology," which emphasizes the psychological experience of grace and forgiveness and freedom from the burden of moral responsibility. Sonship theology teaches that moral striving is always vitiated by hypocrisy. This group embraced their sinfulness, cheerful that, since they could do no good, there was no sense in pretending otherwise. A popular pastor characterized their position as, "Cheer up! You're a lot worse off than you think!"[20]

The traditionalist group identified more strongly with the historical Presbyterian tradition. They also believed in grace and forgiveness, but they stressed that these are spiritual and moral realities more than psychological states. For the traditionalists, it was historic creeds, confessions, and liturgy that defined Presbyterian identity. Both groups were ideologically opposed to Catholicism, but in different ways.

The division between these two camps was real and had political consequences. In the years after I left the school, the "Sonship" group won the battle and initiated a purge. Faculty and staff lost their jobs for not being "grace-minded." To this day, it strikes me as ironic that the "grace" faction is the one that insisted on enforcing ideological purity. Some of the traditionalists eventually left Protestantism and became Catholic.

The theological conflict trickled down to school curricula and pedagogy. The pietists understood classical education as more of a method—an effective way to teach the basics. The traditionalists, however, understood classical studies as initiation into a cultural and intellectual patrimony. These differences were subconscious and rarely expressed, but the fault lines lurked beneath the surface.

The conflict I witnessed in the school leadership was also raging in my own heart. What was the essence of Christian faith? Was it the subjective experience of grace and forgiveness—the

[20]Tullian Tchividjian, *Surprised by Grace: God's Relentless Pursuit of Rebels* (Wheaton, IL: Crossway, 2010), 44.

feeling of being absolutely sure I am going to Heaven? Or was it real, moral, and visible change both in my life and in society? Was it something I could locate privately in my own heart? Or, was the Christian faith an objective, visible reality in the world, expressed in institution and ritual?

I now believe that the conflict I experienced characterizes the whole history of Protestantism. There have been pietist movements and traditionalist reactions in Protestantism since the sixteenth century. The early Reformers emphasized both the psychological experience of grace and forgiveness and the institutional, sacramental dimensions of Christian faith. But, importantly, they also set them in conflict with one another.

This conflict between subjective religion and institutional Christianity played an important role in my ultimate decision to become Catholic. On two occasions that year, my confusion and indecision boiled over, and I realized I would finally have to make a life-changing decision.

* * *

I loved teaching seventh-grade Latin at my school. I saw class as an opportunity to share so much more than nouns and verbs. Latin, for me, was a jumping-off point for teaching all about Western culture, theology, philosophy, history, and literature. I peppered my class with frequent personal anecdotes and allusions to my favorite books and poems. And they seemed to enjoy it: Two went on to university studies in Latin, and one is teaching Latin today. It was one of the most rewarding experiences of my life.

School administration was another matter. I was not even thirty years old when I took the job, and I had never worked in a school before. I knew a lot about Western history and theology, but nothing about grammar-school classrooms. I was wholly unprepared to supervise teachers.

I read and went to conferences to try to get up to speed. At one conference, I met John, a classical-school consultant who eventually played a major role in bringing me to the Catholic Church. I invited him to Birmingham to speak at our annual banquet and to provide in-service training for our teachers. I also invited him to stay with my family at our house. I looked forward to having dinner together and learning more about his life and work.

After dinner, we retired to my living room, and I began to ask John about his life. In talking to him, I started to appreciate that the tensions in our school could be found throughout the Protestant classical-school movement. If you are looking to the past for models of education, you must engage with traditional Catholic education, and if you are looking to ancient tradition, you cannot avoid Catholic tradition. John shocked me when I inquired about his own faith life and he responded that, while he was brought up in a mainstream Protestant denomination, he was thinking of becoming a Catholic. He began to share some of the reading he had been doing and the questions he had been asking about the Faith. It turned out he was raising all the same questions I had, but unlike me, he wasn't drawn to confessional Protestantism. The solution seemed instead to be in the Catholic Church.

That night something earth-shattering happened to me. Up until that point, I had never, ever once considered actually becoming a Catholic. Even though I read Catholic theology and critically investigated the foundations of Protestantism, I was still only seeking for depth and understanding. I never thought I would ever leave the Protestant tradition. Catholicism was a problem to be solved from within my tradition, not a real possibility for me. John was the first person I ever met who seriously considered *becoming Catholic*.

The thought occurred to me for the first time: *I could become Catholic*. I recoiled at the idea, but I also realized something: Every intellectual problem I faced could be resolved in the Catholic Church. There were countless practical difficulties yet to be faced. Theologically, however, I saw that night that Catholicism was a genuine intellectual possibility.

Ironically, John never did enter the Church. We corresponded for a few months after our meeting, but he lost interest in Catholicism. From that first meeting, though, I began to consider seriously the possibility of becoming Catholic. I really, really didn't want to—but I also saw powerful reasons to consider it.

* * *

After my meeting with John, I knew I had to decide one way or the other about Catholicism. I also knew this was no longer simply an academic question, but a spiritual question with profound consequences for my relationship to God and the world. I could not make this decision on my own. I needed supernatural guidance.

As I discussed in the previous chapter, the history of the ancient Church forced me to consider how important the saints are to Christian history and theology. It is not just Roman Catholics who think this: Every Christian tradition with roots in antiquity—that is, everyone but Protestants—believes in the intercession of saints and angels.

This seemed like the time to test the waters. If Catholicism is true, then the intercession of saints and angels is real. I would pray to a saint to ask for help. And there was no question to whom I would pray: It had to be St. Thérèse of Lisieux.

I was terrified—filled with a stomach-churning, primal fear. This is not something that Protestants do. I had been taught that prayers to the saints are really prayers to the Devil: Even if I got an answer, it would be demonic. But if Catholicism were true, then that judgment itself would be "demonic." Jesus warned us never to ascribe to Satan what comes from the Spirit of God. God knew my heart. I had to try.

"St. Thérèse," I prayed, "I am struggling mightily with the question of becoming Catholic. If I am supposed to become a Catholic, please send me a sign. Amen."

I did not really expect an answer—and I certainly did not expect the answer I received. It came during a confrontation about that controversial admissions policy. The event triggered the second turning point for me that year.

We were required to interview all prospective families to ensure that they held the right theology. I handled some of the interviews while board members took others, and it was by God's providence that I interviewed the only two Catholics who applied to the school that year. I never imagined that two living, breathing human beings would walk into my school as emissaries of a saint.

A day or so after I had prayed to St. Thérèse, this couple came to my office to inquire about enrolling their daughter. They had already filled out the application, and I looked over it.

Where the application asked for church affiliation they marked "Roman Catholic."

This is going to be interesting, I thought. I looked at that one personal question we allowed to remain on the paperwork: "If God asked you why He should let you into Heaven, what would you say?" They had written the best answer I had read all year: "Have mercy on me, Lord, a sinner."

They came in my office.

"Welcome," I said, "I'm really glad you're here. Tell me what interests you about our school."

They began to explain their attraction to classical education: They wanted strong academics with a foundation in Western, Christian history and a healthy moral environment with prayer and devotion. I nodded. This is exactly what had attracted me to the place.

"That's good," I said. "Your daughter will get that here. But there is something you need to know about the school as it relates to your Catholicism."

"Oh?" they said.

"Yes," I answered. "There is a very real strain of anti-Catholicism in the school. The curriculum explicitly rejects Catholic belief. Children are taught that Catholics are not Christians, and specifically that the Catholic Church apostatized at the Council of Trent. Do you think you could be comfortable with that emphasis?"

They were genuinely shocked and disappointed.

"Maybe not," they said. "We might have to reconsider."

"I understand," I said. "I also want you to know I appreciate your position. I just want you to know what you'll be in for if you enroll in the school. I am not anti-Catholic myself—in fact, I am quite interested in Catholicism. For instance, I have taken a real liking to St. Thérèse of Lisieux. I have her *Story of a Soul* here on the shelf behind me."

"Oh, that's wonderful!" they answered. "We love St. Thérèse. She is our patroness. We go to St. Thérèse of Lisieux parish!" They went on to describe briefly their love of the Little Flower and of the Catholic Faith.

I was amazed. Up to that point, no Catholic had ever darkened my door—and for the rest of the year, no other Catholics came into our school. But one day after I prayed to St. Thérèse for a sign, two of them walk into my office and identify themselves as her devotees.

This Catholic couple had also given the best answer to the admissions question. Most of the Protestants wrote something like this:

> If God asked me why He should let me into Heaven, I would plead the blood of Christ. I would confess my faith. I would say I'm not worthy, but Christ died for me.

My Catholic couple did not respond with a statement of abstract theology, but with a direct appeal to Christ for mercy. Their position was more immediately grounded in a direct, relational knowledge of Christ than most of the Protestants in my school. I knew their answer also reflected the language of Catholic liturgy. In every Mass, the faithful offer prayers before receiving communion. Two of them stress this personal surrender to Christ's mercy:

"Lamb of God, you take away the sins of the world. Have mercy on us!"

"Lord, I am not worthy that you should enter under my roof, but only say the word and my soul shall be healed."

I asked St. Thérèse for a sign, and she delivered—and it turned out to be the first of two. How do you reconcile inward piety and outward, institutional religion? The answer was literally staring me in the face. I felt sure that Thérèse had answered my prayers.

* * *

I turned a corner in my theological journey that year. Not only did I now feel like Catholicism was a genuine theological and spiritual possibility, but I even began *to desire it*. I found myself driving clandestinely past the local Catholic parish. Sometimes I would pull into the parking lot at night and think about the Blessed Sacrament reserved in a tabernacle in the church.

I felt less and less engaged in Protestant worship or liturgy. I still went to weekly services, but I was intellectually and spiritually aloof; sometimes I would just sit in the "cry room" with a cup of coffee as a critical observer of the ceremony rather than an active participant. As my interest in Protestant worship waned, so did my interest in the work of school administration. I was not yet a Catholic, but I knew that I would have to leave my position. I could no longer carry on in good conscience.

Except for marrying Jill, I have usually been slow to make big decisions. This situation was no different: I didn't know how to move forward. Fortunately, providence guided me in ways beyond my control. The pastor of our church called me into his office one day in the spring semester to discuss the school. It was the only meeting I had with him the entire year, and he asked me kindly but firmly if I thought I was really cut out to be a school administrator.

I was tremendously relieved by the question. I adored teaching, but I was never comfortable as an administrator. Furthermore, my dissertation had gone on hold for a year, and I strongly wanted to finish it. I thought I could get an adjunct teaching job at the local university. Most importantly, I would be free to explore Catholicism.

"You know," I said. "I think I would just be better off doing something else."

The board kindly offered me a job in a purely academic post, teaching Latin and other subjects and relieving me of all administrative duties. I was deeply thankful for the offer, but I knew I couldn't consider it in good conscience. It was time to leave Presbyterianism behind.

Chapter 8

A Very Dark Night

The Catholic Church teaches that grace can be resisted. It is possible to say no to God, even when He calls you.

God was calling me to the Catholic Church. He had sent the saints into my office, so to speak, and He was awakening within me a desire for the Eucharist. I had started looking at Catholicism as more than a possibility. And then I still said no. I didn't resist because I wanted to stay Protestant or because I had any better options. I resisted because I was afraid. I resisted because of what it would cost me to become Catholic.

Grace can be resisted, and when we resist grace, we sometimes end up worse off than when we began. I left the classical school in the spring of 2001 and started teaching courses in Western civilization at the local university. A year later, I still wasn't Catholic; in fact, I wasn't anything. I had lost my faith. I was a nihilist, despairing of any meaning at all. It was the darkest moment in my journey.

* * *

"Jill," I said, "I think I might have to become Catholic."

In the year after I left the classical school, I began opening up to Jill about my theological struggles. She was not pleased.

"David, you're nuts," she said. "You've been reading about this stuff in books. But you don't know anything about real-life Catholics. I grew up Catholic. I know what it's like. Catholics are mean. They don't care about each other. They show up at Mass on Sunday but don't talk to each other. They fight to get out of the parking lot first. Trust me. There's nothing there for you."

Jill made it clear that Catholicism was not an option.

Our marriage was still rocky. The open fights had subsided, but the emotional distance remained. Jill's concerns had turned from the children's physical health to their education. We continued to send them to the classical school for a year after I left, and we also continued to worship at the Presbyterian church. A new divide began to open between us over the question of Catholicism.

How far apart were we? In late October 2001, I traveled to Denver, Colorado, to attend an academic conference, where I delivered a paper on John Calvin. While out of town, I took the opportunity to attend a Catholic Mass. I did not know that back home Jill would also go to Mass that weekend. After hearing me talk about Catholicism, she decided to try Mass again just this once. We had very different experiences.

I went to a parish in downtown Denver, and I remember two things about the liturgy. First, the priest preached a homily about St. Thérèse of Lisieux as an example of reliance upon God's grace. There was an obvious dynamism to his presentation that clearly came from a lived experience of Christ that he shared with the Little Flower, and it seemed perfectly suited to where I was in my spiritual journey.

Second, I remember the feeling that washed over me during the Agnus Dei: "Lamb of God, who takes away the sins of the world, have mercy on us." How could I not think about the Catholic couple who came to my office? How could I not see this as one more grace from God, one more touch from St. Thérèse, and one more invitation to share more fully in the sacraments of the Church?

I was attending a meeting of the very descriptively named Sixteenth Century Studies Society. These gatherings always attract a fair number of Catholics, including Catholic clergy, and in fact I heard from friends that Catholic priests were offering Mass in their hotel rooms. I envied their intimacy with the liturgy and wished that I had been included.

Back in Alabama, Jill had packed up the kids on Sunday morning and took them to the local Catholic parish. When I came home, I got an earful.

"David, it was awful," she said. "It was just like when I was a kid. No one spoke to each other. A woman in front of me had sick kids. They were coughing everywhere. I asked her politely if they could not cough over the back of the pew at my children. She yelled at me! She told me I shouldn't have come to Mass! Then she turned around in a huff. It was cold. It was mean. I was right about Catholics. They're awful. I don't know what I was thinking. I'm never going back. Don't ever ask me again."

There it was. The question was closed. If I wanted any semblance of domestic peace, Catholicism was out of the question. And so I gave up my pursuit of the Church. I said no to grace.

* * *

I turned my attention to my doctoral dissertation, on which I worked obsessively, starting every day at 4:00 a.m. and putting in eight full hours before lunch. No matter what, I was determined to finish the degree. I had put way too much into it to give up now.

The more I studied and wrote about John Calvin, the less sympathetic I was to him. I no longer looked at him as a model theologian or even an exemplary Christian, but just as a brilliant polemicist and a skillful rhetorician. He was a politician, a propagandist, a man with an agenda; I began to regard him from a critical distance as an interesting historical figure who had a powerful cultural impact for better or, more likely, for worse, like Jean-Jacques Rousseau or Karl Marx.

Why does Calvin say what he says? How does his theology serve his political agenda? Who are his enemies? What motivates his reasoning or the questions he chooses to ask and to answer? When I approached Calvin this way, I also started posing similar questions to myself.

Why am I studying Calvin? What motivated me? Why would I consider Catholicism? Am I just a dispassionate seeker of truth? Or am I also pursuing an agenda? Am I just trying to rationalize religious belief to stave off an existential crisis? Was I more interested in theological truth or in climbing the professional ladder within Presbyterianism? Am I looking for God or gratifying my own ego?

My exploration became increasingly philosophical and psychological. How can I know anything true? Is it possible to know anything at all rationally about God, the soul, or the moral life? Why should I even believe the Bible or the Christian tradition? These questions began to torment me almost to madness. I was not thinking anymore about becoming a Catholic; I was wondering whether there was a God. And it was Calvin who pushed me over the edge into this practical atheism.

* * *

Like all the early Protestants, Calvin was compelled to defend the actions and ideologies of the Reformation to his contemporaries. One of his biggest challenges was to defend the Bible itself. After all, the Catholic Church compiled the Bible, determining which texts to include and which to exclude, and so the Reformers necessarily used a Bible handed to them by Catholic tradition. If Protestants were going to reject Catholic tradition, how could they rely on the Bible?

Calvin's answer to this question has become part of the standard arsenal of Protestant apologetics:

> Enlightened by him, we no longer believe, either on our own judgment or that of others, that the Scriptures are from God; but, in a way superior to human judgment, feel perfectly assured—as much so as if we beheld the divine image visibly impressed on it—that it came to us, by the instrumentality of men, from the very mouth of God.... We feel a divine energy living and breathing in it—an energy by which we are drawn and animated to obey it, willingly indeed, and knowingly, but more vividly and effectually than could be done by human will or knowledge.[21]

Protestant theologians refer to this subjective experience of spooky feelings while reading Scripture as the "witness of the Holy Spirit," and it plays a very important role in Protestant theology. Whenever it comes to first principles—God, the inspiration of Scripture, the biblical canon—Calvinist theologians fall back on this "witness of the Spirit." In one sense, it is really a brilliant answer, at least polemically: I can claim to have had any purely interior experience, and no one can ever contradict me. And those who think they've had the same interior experience can form themselves into a moral community distinct from those on the outside who do not have the Spirit.

I accepted this answer for most of my life, but now I was questioning it. Was this really a good reason to believe in the Bible, or God, or anything? Reading Calvin, I raised again the most fundamental question of all about the Christian faith: How do I know that any of it is true?

[21] *Institutes of the Christian Religion*, trans. Ford Lewis Battles, ed. John T. McNeill, 2 vols. (Philadelphia: Westminster Press, 1960), 1.7.5.

I don't remember the precise date, but I do remember where I was when I lost my faith completely. I was sitting at a desk in my parents' house reading Calvin when the question came to me: "Can I claim to know anything objective about the world from a purely interior and private experience?"

As soon as I raised the question, I saw in a flash that the answer had to be no. I might have an experience, but the interpretation of that experience is not at all obvious, and so the only thing I can know with certainty is, simply, "I have had an experience." It does not matter how intense the spooky feelings might be: They can't prove that the Bible comes from God.

And as I considered my own history, I realized that I had not actually come to believe in Scripture because of religious experience; I believed in the Bible *because my parents and teachers told me to*. To this day, there are books of the Bible that leave me cold—in which I don't feel a "divine energy living and breathing"—and there are plenty of nonbiblical books that move me much more profoundly on an emotional level. To this day, *The Chronicles of Narnia*, especially the end of *The Last Battle*, moves me to tears. Some days I feel as if I can relate to Luke Skywalker more than to Moses.

I saw that Calvin was simply engaged in after-the-fact rationalization. Luther set the agenda for Protestants by appealing to Scripture and rejecting sacred Tradition. The work of justifying that conclusion came later—to propagandists such as John Calvin.

Apart from "the witness of the Spirit," I knew of no other definitive reason for believing in Scripture or God. And should I even seek for "reasons"? If I try to justify my preexisting religious belief, am I not doing the same thing Calvin did? Isn't that just rationalization? As I saw it, there could be no rationally compelling reason to believe in God or not to believe in God. I was lost.

Jill saw me wandering the house. She could tell that something was wrong.

"What's going on with you?" she asked.

"Jill, I'm losing my faith."

She knew I had been struggling with Protestantism. But this was something different.

"But you still believe in God?" she asked. "You believe in Jesus?"

"I don't know."

Her face fell, and her eyes widened with shock.

"Oh!" she said. "Oh."

She didn't know what else to say.

For ten years, I had poured my life into studying my faith. It had cost us a decade of lost opportunities, endless hours apart, and no immediate prospects for the future. We were hopelessly distant from one another. And the result was only that I had systematically demolished the intellectual foundations of my childhood religion.

Justification by faith? Out the window.

Scripture alone? Gone.

The truth of the Bible, the existence of God, the person of Christ—who can know about these things? I didn't know where to turn.

* * *

One day I was a Presbyterian with problems, drawn to Catholicism but unsure what to do. The next day I was nothing, an anguished agnostic who did not know whether there was a God, let alone which version of Christianity might be true.

You might think the collapse of my Protestant faith would drive me immediately into the Catholic Church, but it didn't work that way. Instead, it destroyed my faith altogether. Protestantism was the scaffolding I stood on while exploring the edifice of Catholicism. Initially, I had compared the two traditions *as a Christian trying to make sense of my faith*. But when the world of Protestantism vanished completely, I had to confront a question I had not anticipated: *Why be a Christian at all?*

Catholicism presented many beautiful truths and lofty ideals. But could it be true *as a whole*? And how would I know? The main contours of the faith—belief in God, in Christ, and in the Bible—were things I accepted largely based on subjective religious experience and the testimony of trusted mentors. If I had warm feelings from prayer or from the courageous example of missionaries, I associated those feelings with the guidance or witness of the Holy Spirit. Now this seemed naïve to me.

I needed to think through Christianity from the ground up. But how should I start? I hardly knew where to begin, and I despaired of finding any sure foothold—anything I could know for certain. I had been sincere in my Protestantism, but very, very wrong. Like a young person who had gone through a tempestuous breakup, I was wary about committing myself to anything again.

And so I gave up the quest for truth for a year. I didn't just give up exploring Catholicism; I gave up the practice of religion entirely. Instead, I concentrated on finishing the degree that had cost me so much. I spent time with my children. I tried to plan financially for my family's growing needs. That all kept me busy, but I had suffered a profound spiritual loss.

In my anguish, I turned to meditation and to fiction, especially science fiction and fantasy. I simply wanted to get away from philosophy and theology. I wanted to escape from this quest for a certainty that was likely impossible ever to satisfy.

During this phase of my life, no religion appealed to me more than Buddhism. I didn't think Buddhism was "true," but I found it useful—more a program for self-help and mental calm than a set of truth claims. I also read a good deal of Chaim Potok, a Jewish writer whose experiences somewhat paralleled my own. Most of his novels depict anguished characters who are torn between two traditions. In his best works, Potok does not resolve these conflicts; instead, his characters suffer but gain insight as they are crushed between competing worldviews. Most days I felt like just such a character.

I also finally decided to give up on a career in academia. I loved the work—poring over texts, walking the library stacks, lecturing to students—but it was going to cost me and my family too dearly. I knew what was in store if I kept at it: years on the tenure treadmill, more cross-country moves, and hours in libraries away from my family—all for very little pay. I determined to finish my degree, but I also began to look for work in a new field.

* * *

There are people who experience the loss of faith as a liberation. Others find it existentially disorienting. For some, faith simply fades into irrelevance, and they barely feel its loss.

According to William James, a religious person believes that there is an unseen order in the universe and that the aim of life is to bring one's life into harmony with that order. I think that is the best definition of religion I have found. Not everyone finds the idea of an unseen order appealing, but to me, the idea has always been as real as the nose on my face and a good bit more attractive.

The world without faith felt hollowed out to me. It was just a world of brute facts, of unintelligible objects. Shakespeare talks about life as "a poor player that struts and frets his hour upon the stage." It felt like that to me—as if I were only playing at life while I observed myself from the outside. The objects of my experience were just props and my choices but a fiction; my life was no more meaningful than Macbeth's.

Even Buddhism, which of all the non-Western religions I have always found the most interesting, seemed like a big, silly game. The life of the Buddha, the Four Noble Truths, the Eightfold Path—no more real or unreal than Luke Skywalker, and a good deal less real than Narnia.

Amazingly, it ended up being Jill who pushed me to take up again the pursuit of the Catholic Faith. She witnessed my soul dying within me, the collapse of my spiritual energies, and the loss of my moral compass. I had stopped praying. I continued to go to Sunday services with my family, but she could see that I was utterly disengaged. I spoke to my children about courage, fortitude, nobility, and the moral life, but my words lacked conviction. Instead of turning to Scripture, I drew examples from pop culture. "What would Obi-wan Kenobi do?" I asked.

"David," Jill said. "You've got to quit talking to the kids about *Star Wars*. You've got to talk to them about God, about Christ."

Jill's own spiritual life was just as anemic as mine. She hardly believed, no longer prayed, and pushed me more to make money than to practice the faith. But she could not bear for her children to grow up in a cold, empty universe. And like me, she couldn't shake her attraction to Jesus.

* * *

Jill and Jesus drew me back to the search for faith by forcing me to take a stand for reality, for love, and for a life of meaning.

Calvinism had not simply cost me my faith; it had deformed my whole approach to reality. Like the French philosopher René Descartes, Calvinism is radically skeptical about human experience: Can I trust my moral judgments? My philosophical reasoning? Even my own senses? Descartes decided he should doubt everything except his own conscious existence: "I think. Therefore, I am." Calvinism does something similar. In Calvinism, humans are so corrupt that they can trust nothing about their own experience except the "witness of the Spirit." Like Descartes, Calvinists turn within looking for certainty.

Calvinism taught me to divorce my inner world from the outer world. I could know myself through the Spirit, but what about *out there*? This disintegration contributed to my sense of unreality: I could regard myself from the outside, like an object wandering around without meaning or purpose, or I could look out at the world as through a window, while empty phenomena passed by. However, I could not reach through the glass and lay hold of anything substantial. I acted in the world, but without conviction—with less conviction even than Macbeth's poor player strutting about the stage.

But in truth we cannot shut off our encounter with reality, nor can we eliminate the fact that this encounter is meaningful. Even if I shut myself off from everyone and assert that everything is meaningless, I cannot stop being in relation to others. I am acting still significantly in the world even if I meditate quietly with my eyes closed: My children and wife and friends and neighbors do not simply disappear and stop needing me. I can choose *how* to engage, but not *whether* to engage. And I cannot be neutral in the question of how to engage with the world: Not to decide is to decide. So, what should I do?

Dag Hammarskjöld, former secretary-general of the UN, faced a similar crisis. It is possible to say yes or no to reality—including the reality of God—but we must say one or the other. Hammarskjöld decided to say yes:

> I didn't know Who—or what—put the question, I don't know when it was put. I don't even remember answering. But at some moment I did answer Yes to Someone and from that hour I was certain that existence is meaningful and that, therefore, my life, in self-surrender, had a goal.[22]

[22]Dag Hammarskjöld, *Markings*, trans. Leif Sjöbert and W. H. Auden (New York: Knopf, 1964), xi.

Jill and Jesus both forced me to ask this question anew. How would I regard my life? Would I take responsibility for my being in the world, and for its significance? I wanted philosophical answers to my questions, and I did not want to decide before I had them. Jill and Jesus both refused to engage me in that way. I forgave Jill that oversight, but Jesus angered me. Shouldn't He answer my questions? But instead of answering, He put the question to me: "What will you say to me?"

I have always found Jesus tremendously frustrating in this way. He almost never answers questions directly. He offers no rigorous philosophical account of Christian faith, though His teaching is not without philosophical significance. He presents not so much an argument to be evaluated as a way of being in the world—an invitation to share in His way of seeing, loving, and choosing.

When I meet a person socially, I don't see him as an argument or a thesis, but as an encounter—a possibility of new relationship that opens transcendent horizons. When I make a friend, his life opens to me: His interests, loves, passions, and sorrows become mine. He may challenge me with philosophy, but that is not what friendship with him *means*. Friendship means caring about my friend and caring about what matters to my friend. As with any other person, coming to terms with Jesus means coming to terms with the possibility of friendship more than it does assenting to a philosophy.

Pope Benedict XVI describes the encounter this way:

> Being Christian is not the result of an ethical choice or a lofty idea, but the encounter with an event, a person, which gives life a new horizon and a decisive direction.[23]

[23] Benedict XVI, encyclical letter *Deus Caritas Est* (December 25, 2005), no. 1.

Jesus' way of being in the world is unique. His orientation toward law, love, and truth has fascinated the world for two thousand years. There are, from a human point of view, better philosophers—or at least there are thinkers who give more rigorously argued, articulate, systematic answers. But no one has had a greater, more lasting, or more beneficial impact on humanity than Jesus.

And the Catholic Church is the most tangible expression of Christ's presence in the world. Jesus called His apostles and then sent them out to form a society. That society has been going for two thousand years and is as manifest, evident, and present today as is New York City. Its shape, form, and action—especially in liturgy—is an immediate echo of Jesus' life, death, and Resurrection. I don't have to imagine a distant past to encounter Jesus, and I don't have to look within to a purely interior and subjective experience. The experience is right in front of me in the Catholic Church. The only remaining question is: Will I join?

When someone throws you a baseball and it's coming right at you, you don't have to wonder if the pitcher really exists, and you don't pause to consider whether the ball is real. The ball is about to smash you in the head. What will you do? Will you catch, duck, or stand there? Jesus threw a fast ball down two thousand years, and it was barreling down on me. What would I do?

There was only one real option not available to me. I could not say, "Life is meaningless, but I will act as if it is meaningful." Humans cannot simply act from instinct without reflection. We always act with some conception of reality, even if it's a skeptical one. I had to make a decision for or against reality—more precisely, I had to make a decision for or against Jesus, and therefore I had to make a decision for or against the Church.

I knew on some level that I owed it to Jesus, whoever He was, and to my family not to give up the quest for truth and meaning.

Chapter 9

Becoming Catholic

"You should just go ahead and become a Catholic," Jill said.

"Are you serious?" I asked. "You can't stand the Catholic Church."

"No, I can't. But it's where your heart is. I see that. You need this. We need it."

I would never have become a Catholic without my wife. I would never have studied theology, confronted the depths of my own spiritual need, or sought cures for my moral weakness without the duty that I knew I owed her as a husband. The Catholic Church would eventually save my marriage, but marriage saved me for the Catholic Church.

Jill still wanted no part of the Catholic Church. But she also saw that Catholicism had become the center of my moral imagination. The Church enlivened my spiritual and intellectual energies. For me, to think of God, Christ, or the moral life was to become absorbed in the Catholic ethos. Each time I turned away from Catholicism, I felt morally and spiritually drained, weakened, and lost.

Jill has been the driving force at most of the critical junctures of my life. I tend to live a very abstracted life, questioning and theorizing about almost everything while finding it difficult to make concrete decisions. My wife, by contrast, is more interested in solutions than in investigating problems.

Jill was the one who decided to transfer to a Christian college, and then she was the one who decided to leave college, which prompted me to propose marriage. A few years later, Jill was the one who first urged children. Jill was not invested in the truth or falsehood of Catholicism because she could find no comfort or encouragement for herself in the Church—but she saw that it had become necessary for me. And so Jill was the one who urged me to take up again the move toward Catholicism.

My wife's prompting has been for me one of the great goods of marriage. Jill keeps me grounded in the real. This is something that Catholic tradition has observed. In his encyclical on marriage, *Casti Connubii*, Pope Pius XI argued that women excel their husbands in love—and love is not abstract, but concrete. It is care for *this* person in *this* circumstance. Pope John Paul II, furthermore, argued that there is a feminine genius—a unique "sensitivity for human beings in every circumstance: because they are human!—and because 'the greatest of these is love!'"[24]

Jill was pushing me to become a Catholic—but now I resisted. Why would I hold back? I was still deeply tormented by philosophical questions about God and about truth itself, and I did not want to commit myself irrationally. The Catholic Faith might be ancient, beautiful, and inspiring—but is it true? I did not know how to think about these questions, let alone how to answer them. Ultimately, I found my answer in St. Thomas Aquinas and in an analogy drawn from Scripture. In a way, appropriately enough, I found my answer in marriage.

[24] John Paul II, apostolic letter *Mulieris Dignitatem* (August 15, 1988), no. 30.

* * *

The work of St. Thomas Aquinas (1225–1274) is the definitive expression of Catholic reflection on the relationship between faith and reason. I had read Thomas as a graduate student before I was interested in becoming Catholic, but only to fill in gaps in my knowledge of Catholic history. Now I read Thomas for spiritual insight.

The first thing I learned from St. Thomas was that I had been thinking the wrong way about faith. I thought I had abandoned my Calvinism, but I saw in reading St. Thomas that I had been thinking about faith like a Calvinist and not like a Catholic.

Calvinists talk about faith as something that happens *to* you, not something you have any agency in whatsoever. For the Calvinist, faith does not come from proofs or arguments, but only from the direct action of the Holy Spirit. God just makes you see that the faith is true. Furthermore, Calvinists teach that God's action cannot be resisted: If He acts on you to give you faith, you are going to have faith. And that's that.

Catholics understand faith differently. In Catholic doctrine, faith is a human act—a decision we make to believe what God has revealed about Himself. Now, God certainly helps the soul to believe. I don't believe without God's help, but believing remains something that I do. Faith is not a "blind impulse of the mind," but a considered judgment that Christ and the Church are credible and trustworthy.

The Bible compares our relationship to God to human marriage, an analogy that helps us understand something about the relationship between faith and reason. Marriage can be a very rational decision, but it still takes trust. If a man decides that his fiancée is trustworthy, then getting married is very reasonable. But how can I find out if my fiancée is trustworthy? I can find reasons to trust my fiancée, but in the end, it's not the sort of thing I can demonstrate with a mathematical proof. In the end, I must decide whether to trust her and get married based on the available evidence. The Catholic Church says faith is like that. There are good reasons for faith, but in the end, *you must still decide.*

Why does this difference matter? As a Presbyterian, it was very important for me to say that "I knew for sure" about everything: "Are you sure you are going to Heaven? Are you sure that you are saved? Are you sure the Bible is God's word? Are you sure there is a God?" In all these cases, the Calvinist might consult rational arguments, but ultimately, he trusts the "witness of the Spirit." In the end, his certainty comes from subjective religious experience.

In my formation as a Calvinist, I had developed the habit of identifying my emotional life with the activity of the Holy Spirit. But I was growing to doubt this idea of the "witness of the Spirit." I didn't know if I could be "sure" ever again. Without that certainty, I did not see how I could ever commit myself to a religious tradition. This is where Thomas helped me the most.

Thomas helped me see that the content of Christian faith can really be divided into two categories: There are things that we can know with certainty from reason and argument, and there are things that we believe simply on the authority of Christ and the Church. Furthermore—and this is important—there are *good reasons* to trust Christ and the Church. We do not *just believe*. These distinctions are very important to understanding what faith should feel like, or whether it should feel like anything at all.

Authentic Catholic philosophers such as St. Thomas work very hard to prove parts of the Christian faith, but they also admit freely that we can accept other parts only on authority. The Calvinists I studied with did not divide the content of the faith in this way. They considered the faith as a whole, and they dismissed purely philosophical accounts of God, the soul, or the moral life. They were not just uninterested in proving the content of even one part of Christian faith but were skeptical that setting out to do so could be valuable at all.

* * *

I recall the very text that changed my mind about becoming Catholic. Here is the essential passage from Thomas's *De veritate* (*On Truth*):

> We are moved to believe what God says because we are promised eternal life as a reward if we believe. And this reward moves the will to assent to what is said, although the intellect is not moved by anything which it understands. Therefore, Augustine says: "Man can do other things unwillingly, but he can believe only if he wills it." (14.1)

In one sense, I felt a tremendous disappointment when I read this text. I saw in a flash what St. Thomas was challenging me to do: take responsibility for my belief or unbelief. I could wait a lifetime for God to compel me to believe—and I would likely die without faith. Or I could also respond freely to His invitation to believe. It was disappointing because I realized that I could never achieve the kind of certainty that comes from an immediate and intuitive experience. But it was also liberating, because I finally saw clearly that this is not a bad thing.

When I read this passage, I had an epiphany more powerful than the loss I felt on the day my faith first slipped away. I saw clearly how faith could be a *rational possibility* without being *rationally compelled*.

Again, it was rather like marriage. It is not irrational to marry a woman, especially one who has demonstrated her trustworthiness. Does my wife really love me? Will she be faithful forever? Can we get over our conflicts and make a life together? What will happen if I apologize? Will she forgive me? Can I ever be happy with this woman? These questions all have answers, but they are not the sort of thing that admit of mathematical certainty.

Catholicism is similarly an invitation to a kind of relationship and a way of being in the world. Above all, I think Catholicism is an invitation to believe that our moral convictions and our desire for meaning correspond to something real—something, or rather Someone, so real that He became incarnate in the world, taking on flesh in the womb of a virgin. You can't get more real than that.

There are good reasons to believe in the Incarnation; Catholic theology calls them the "motives of credibility." The fulfillment of prophecy, the miracles of Christ, His Resurrection, and the profound moral influence of Catholicism on world history all testify to the truth of Christian claims. Do these reasons compel me to believe? Obviously they do not; there are many people who consider these reasons and still do not have faith. I must choose what position I will take on life, and whether to accept or to resist the arguments in favor of Christ.

The great existential challenge in the world today is whether there is any meaning at all. Childlessness, suicide, and euthanasia are depopulating whole societies that have given up on life and prefer to die quietly in bed. Japan now sells more adult diapers than baby diapers. Russia has more abortions than live births.

Where would I stand? Is there any truth? Is there any love that endures? Every fiber of my being said yes. Yes, to reason; yes, to love; yes, to hope; yes, even to suffering.

I knew I had to become a Catholic.

* * *

"Father, I think I may need to become a Catholic."

In fall of 2003, I made an appointment to meet Msgr. Martin Muller at Our Lady of Sorrows Church in Homewood, Alabama. Fr. Muller was kind and very solicitous about my soul, my family life, and my faith in God.

"Are you marrying a Catholic? Or have you read your way into the Church?"

I'll never forget that question for as long as I live. For fifteen years, I have thought long and hard about what this says about the Catholic Church. I have met many converts to and from Catholicism in my life, and very, very few of them read their way *out of* the Church. The general pattern, if I'm being honest, is that poorly formed Catholics become Protestants. And well-formed Protestants become Catholics.

At the same time, few people simply walk into a local parish and convert. The Catholic tradition is ancient, deep, and comparatively complex. It is difficult to swallow the whole thing in one bite. So Fr. Muller knew that my decision to become Catholic must have been motivated by some very serious soul-searching. It was not a casual response to the Fourth of July Festival, even though Our Lady of Sorrows is famous for its festival!

Fr. Muller began to ask me about my faith, my life, and my family. I told him I was not yet certain about the Catholic Faith and that I was still trying to make up my mind.

"What about the motives of credibility?" he asked.

"What about the motives of incredibility?" I asked. He laughed when I said that.

Father handed me a copy of his own book on the motives of credibility. I appreciated his concern and was glad to have found a priest who took these questions seriously.

"What about your moral obligation to worship God?" he asked.

This one struck me. Father's question was a perfectly sensible one. It is a consistent part of Scripture, Catholic tradition, and a good deal of ancient philosophy that we owe some form of reverence to the Supreme Being. But, honestly, I had never thought of it before. So much of the "gospel" I grew up with was an answer to the question "What's in it for me?" But that's really the wrong place to start. A better question is "What is the right thing to do?"

He asked me about my religious background, and I explained that I had grown up Protestant, gone to Protestant college and seminary, and had just recently earned my Ph.D. in historical theology. I told him I had studied the history of Catholic theology extensively, read the Fathers and the Doctors of the Church, and had just finished reading the *Catechism of the Catholic Church.*

"You read the whole *Catechism?*" he asked.

"Yep, the whole thing."

"Well, you certainly don't need to wait until Easter. We can bring you in a lot sooner."

Up until that point, I had a strong inclination to become a Catholic, but not a definite plan. Fr. Muller's offer put the decision to me forcefully. *Am I going to become a Catholic or not?*

We decided on Sunday afternoon, November 16, for me to be received into the Church. We also planned to have my fourth child, Justin Dominic, baptized at the same time.

Finally, Father said, "You will need to go to confession sometime before then. You don't have to make an appointment if you don't want to. Just find any priest in the confessional and tell him what's up."

This is where it got real.

I was going to go to confession. I had lived in a kind of fascinated horror of the confessional all my life. Passing through the door would mark the major sacramental transformation of my life. It was the beginning of everything.

* * *

On a Saturday afternoon a few weeks after that first meeting, I got in line for confession at Our Lady of Sorrows.

"Father," I said. "I'm becoming a Catholic in a few weeks. I've never done this before. I'm not sure what I'm doing. Would it be okay if I just went through the Ten Commandments and examined my life?"

He said that would be fine.

I went down the commandments like a list, checking them off. The priest raised his eyebrows when I confessed to idolatry.

"What exactly do you mean by idolatry?" he asked.

"When I was in high school," I replied, "I really felt like I worshipped rock and roll. I kept posters of rock bands on my wall almost in veneration. Fame, pleasure, and autonomy were my idols."

"Oh, that makes sense."

It was probably a pretty poor first confession. I imagine I could have done a better examination of conscience. What I remember most, however, were the words of absolution, which assert that God forgave my sins "through the ministry of the Church." This priest was not claiming to forgive my sins by his own authority, but as an emissary of the Church, the Body of Christ, to whom Jesus gave the power to speak and act in His name. "He who hears you hears me," He said (Luke 10:16). "If you forgive the sins of any, they are forgiven" (John 20:23).

The other thing that struck me was the glorious objectivity of the promise. The claim to forgive sins was grounded in the objective words of Christ, not in the subjective faith of the penitent. This was important because when I was a Protestant, I was accustomed to thinking of the sacraments as merely symbolic. As symbols only, they taught general truths that applied to every believer: For instance, the washing of baptism symbolized forgiveness of sins, and the Lord's Supper symbolized His death for us on the Cross. But how would I know that these truths applied to me personally?

Calvinists believe notoriously that Christ did not die for everyone, and therefore that the sacraments do not work for everyone. When a Calvinist approaches a sacrament, he must ask, "How do I know this symbol applies *to me*?" The only way he can answer this question is to look within and to decide whether he has "true faith."

The Calvinist is faced with a dilemma. If I am elect—if I am really saved—then I can have infallible certainty of my salvation.

But many people claim to have such assurance and subsequently fall away. It is possible to be *deceived* about the state of my salvation, and so the nagging question never goes away: Maybe my faith really isn't "true faith." I heard a former Protestant minister explain the dilemma this way: "The elect know for sure that they are going to Heaven, and I might be one of them." The promise of "absolute assurance" fails.

Catholics believe that the sacraments are symbols, yes, but also that they are much more. A mere symbol teaches only a general truth that applies to many, but a sacrament touches me *personally*. The priest does not say, "I declare forgiveness of sins to all who believe," but rather, "I declare that your sins are forgiven, David Anders, and I do so with the authority of Christ."

The day of my first confession, I realized that the Catholic Church has the best and only answer to the problem of assurance. I do not need and can never construct complete assurance on the shifting sands of my own subjective experience. I have absolute assurance instead in the objective word of Christ's promise, which is that grace is to be found in the sacraments. If I stay with the sacraments, I know for sure that I am placing myself in the path of grace. What I need to do now is persevere until the end.

I was not expecting the experience to be so powerful, but I walked out of the confessional that day truly a changed man. I do not mean that I quit sinning—far from it. But I left the confessional with an entirely different perspective on life, holiness, guilt, forgiveness, and religious psychology.

The confessional was incredibly healing to my reason, to my sanity, and to my emotions. I saw in a flash that I had lived my religious life up to that point as an actor, a pretender, an impostor. I had spent my life pretending to know things I could not know, such as the truth of my salvation and that the Holy Spirit directly guided my emotions. These are the kinds of beliefs that lead to fanaticism, intolerance, and crushing disillusionment. The confessional relieved me of an enormous psychological burden. It was not just the burden of guilt, but the burden of having to know for sure that I was elect, predestined, or saved.

The confessional also prepared me for the sacrament of sacraments—the Source and Summit of the Catholic life in which the truth of salvation touches me most directly and most personally. "Whoever eats my flesh and drinks my blood abides in me," Jesus said (John 6:56). Here, more than in my fleeting emotions and subjective states of mind, I could find the greatest assurance of salvation.

* * *

On November 16, 2003, I gathered at Our Lady of Sorrows Parish with my wife and children, a few friends, and Fr. Muller.

Father baptized my fourth child, Justin, who was eight months old at the time. I was impressed that the Rite of Baptism is considerably longer in the Catholic Church than in the Presbyterian tradition. The solemnity of the rite gives one a powerful sense of entering into a new, supernatural state.

Next, I was to receive the sacrament of Confirmation—but before that I had to make a profession of faith in the Catholic Church. The content of that profession has never left me. Like my first confession, it was a moment of profound psychological transformation.

This is what I recited:

> I believe and profess all that the holy Catholic Church believes, teaches, and proclaims to be revealed by God.

Why was this so powerful? Some people think that Catholics surrender their intellect and trust blindly to whatever the pope or their priest has to say, but that is a profound misunderstanding.

The Catholic does not promise to believe the pope, the bishop, or the priest. He promises only to believe everything that the Church has defined solemnly as having been revealed by God. Far from constraining the intellect, this has a profoundly liberating effect on the mind. It enables the believer to take a thoroughly critical stance toward religious discourse without surrendering essential objective truths.

Protestants do not clearly distinguish dogma from opinion. As a Protestant, I felt the need to be certain, but what (and whom) exactly I was certain about shifted all the time. The last persuasive preacher, book, or clever idea provided my "certainty," which I was "sure" to find justified somewhere in the Bible. This is not the attitude of a critically minded person, but that of a credulous and naïve person, "tossed to and fro and carried about with every wind of doctrine, by the cunning of men, by their craftiness in deceitful wiles" (Eph. 4:14).

As a Catholic, I suddenly gained the freedom to be authentically critical of myself, of ideology, and even of religious leaders. I could clearly distinguish dogmas from private opinions, allowing me to surrender the right to determine the former, but to gain the right to be ruthlessly critical of the latter. I was instantly free from a thousand pious platitudes.

After my profession, Fr. Muller anointed my forehead with oil and prayed, "Be sealed with the gift of the Holy Spirit."

Why is this sacrament necessary? What did I gain?

As a Protestant, I associated the Holy Spirit with the ups and downs of my everyday emotional life. Many times, I have heard Protestants speak of a religious service or time in prayer when "they felt the Spirit." I think they felt no such thing. I think what they felt were lively religious emotions. But Jesus says, "You cannot tell where the Spirit comes from or where it is going" (see John 3:8).

There is a prayer in the Mass—Eucharistic Prayer II—wherein the priest asks God to send His Spirit upon the elements "like the dewfall." The dew comes silently upon the grass, and the Spirit can also come silently into our lives—but He brings great effects.

The Church tells me that my whole life of faith from start to finish has been the work of the Spirit of God. My agonies, sorrows, struggles, hopes, and disappointments led me to the Church more surely than my religious emotions. My profession of faith itself, though fraught with emotional consequences, was not an emotional decision, but a carefully considered judgment.

With my senses, I felt nothing but oil on my forehead when I was confirmed, but I knew something far more powerful was happening. I knew that God had promised to send His Spirit into my life in a new and powerful way. He would now give me grace to bear witness to the Catholic Faith, but in ways I could not anticipate.

* * *

Whatever Jesus wants us to do, He represents to us in a sacrament. He wants us to die to ourselves and be reborn in Him; hence baptism. He wants us to seek forgiveness and to be forgiving; hence reconciliation. He wants us to know we have been sealed by the Spirit and equipped for ministry; hence confirmation. Above all, He wants us to abide in Him, to draw nourishment from Him, and to be rebuilt and reformed in Him day by day in the closest possible communion. Could you represent this more intimately than by ingestion, by the Eucharist?

In the Catholic Church, abiding in Christ is a *dynamic* activity. Christ touches you at a point in time, but His influence grows and deepens throughout life. Constant contact with the source of grace is necessary. "Abide in me as I abide in you," Jesus says. "Just as the branch cannot bear fruit by itself unless it abides in the vine, neither can you, unless you abide in me" (John 15:4). The sacrament of this "abiding" is the Holy Eucharist.

In my Protestant life, I understood the Eucharist simply as a symbol of Christ's death on the Cross. Communion reminded me of what had been done in the past, and salvation was a one-time event, both in the sense of taking place once and for all on Calvary and in the sense of being realized once in my life, at the moment of conversion.

In the evangelical world, there is a lot of emphasis on identifying the precise moment of conversion. The popular question is: "When did you become a Christian?" What that means is: "When were you converted? When did you 'pray to receive Christ' or decide to turn your life over to Jesus?" In some denominations, it is this critical moment of conversion that constitutes full initiation into the faith.

The Catholic Faith recognizes the deeply human truth that conversion is a process. The Catholic Church recognizes three sacraments of initiation: baptism, confirmation, and Communion. We do not "become a Christian" through the sinner's prayer, by "inviting Jesus into my life," or by responding to an altar call. We become a Christian through baptism. "All who have been baptized have clothed themselves with Christ" (see Gal. 3:27). It is in the Holy Eucharist, however, that we partake fully in the life and grace of the Catholic Church. "Because there is one bread, we who are many are one body, for we all partake of the one bread" (1 Cor. 10:17).

I did not receive Communion in the Catholic Church until the Sunday after my confirmation, at a regular parish Mass. That is when the significance of what I had done fully hit me. I was not elated or excited in the least. Rather, I felt nervous and confused and a bit disappointed that there was not more fanfare. I simply got in line for Communion with everyone else.

The Catholic Faith can indeed be very emotional. However, the real significance of the Faith is not in the emotional life but in the reason and the will. There was no pomp and circumstance when

I received the Eucharist. There were no bright lights or exploding canons. But there was something far more important. There was a reasoned, willful decision to plant my flag, to order my life, and to declare my unity with Christ's Body, the Church. I accepted the yoke. I yielded, not to an emotional decision or to an altar call, but to a life of ongoing communion with the Body of Christ.

I received the Sacred Host and thought, "I did it. I'm really a Catholic."

* * *

What was the significance of becoming Catholic as far as my marriage was concerned?

At each stage of my journey toward Catholicism, I learned to trust myself less and to rely more on God's wisdom and grace. Catholics find that wisdom and grace expressed visibly in the Church, Her sacraments, Her traditions, and the objective order of nature and reason.

For the Catholic, what matters is not what I feel, but what is right and just and true. The promise of the gospel, for a Catholic, is that God will bring my life into accord with the right, the just, and the true—provided I cooperate with His grace.

This is very different from life as a Protestant. Consider what the Lutheran Augsburg Confession says about saving faith:

> Men ... are freely justified for Christ's sake, through faith, when they believe they are received into favor. (art. 4)

In the Lutheran tradition, believing that I am saved makes me saved. This is not at all what faith is like for a Catholic. When a Catholic says, "I believe," he is not saying, "I believe I am saved." He is saying, "Christ died to save me. God offers me His grace. If I cooperate with that grace and persevere until the end, then I will be saved."

What does it take to persevere to the end as a Catholic? Jesus said, "Whoever does not bear his own cross and come after me, cannot be my disciple" (Luke 14:27). Paradoxically, the good news of salvation is that we are called to suffer. But it is not as bad as it sounds. We are bound to suffer anyway, whether we believe or not. What the gospel promises, beautifully, is that God will redeem our suffering, that our suffering can have meaning.

Becoming a Catholic reoriented my life and my priorities away from myself, my experiences, and my personal satisfaction and toward an objective conception of the good—especially the good of marriage. I do not mean to say that my will and affections immediately followed suit. Becoming Catholic did not immediately make me holy or virtuous, but it changed the way I viewed and acted in the world.

My wife urged me to become a Catholic, but she did not yet share my faith. It was a concession, not a shared conviction. And so our marriage was still difficult. We were still distant, though we were united in support of the welfare of our children. The decision to baptize Justin as a Catholic was an important move toward a common life, but disappointment lurked right around the corner.

Chapter 10

Growing Pains

Jill and I lived largely separate religious lives for four years.

After I was received into the Church, I urged Jill to practice the Catholic Faith. As a cradle Catholic, all that was necessary for her to return to the Faith was to go to confession. And, once, she did. It was a disaster.

When she came out of the confessional, I could see at a glance that she was angry.

"Do you know what that priest told me?" she said.

"What?"

"I told him my sins, and he said, 'What about the sin of not going to Mass for all those years?' He was so judgmental. I'll never go to confession again."

Any encouragement Jill gave me in my Catholic faith vanished at that point. The Faith became a battleground.

"Can we pray the Rosary together?"

"No."

"Will you come to Mass?"

"No."

Despite all this, Jill did allow me to enroll our oldest child, Jonathan, in a Catholic School run by Dominican Sisters in the fall of 2004. She appreciated at some level that Catholicism could do something positive for her children. A few of the sisters took an interest in Jonathan, and their prayers and personal interventions were clearly meaningful both to him and to Jill.

* * *

For four years, my greatest comfort in life was the confessional. However, my parish's scheduled Saturday confession time proved to be impossible for me: It meant leaving Jill to care for our four children for what she considered to be my personal religious pastimes, and she didn't like it one bit. I had to find another time to go to confession.

As providence would have it, I bought a home five miles away from EWTN, the largest Catholic broadcaster in the world. Although I had grown up in Birmingham, I had no idea that EWTN was in my backyard, but once I learned about it, I quickly saw this would be a good place to grow in my secret sacramental life. The chapel on the network's campus offered confessions every day of the week, so I could go there during my lunch hour and Jill would never know.

In addition to the television and radio studios, the EWTN campus houses a friary staffed with Franciscan priests and brothers. They maintain a rich liturgical life for the network's employees and the many pilgrims who visit the studios daily from around the world. The Mass, the Liturgy of the Hours, Eucharistic adoration, Rosaries, devotions, and confessions punctuate the day. A Catholic bookstore offers a rich supply of catechetical and theological materials. Once I discovered EWTN, I was hooked.

The greatest blessing to me at EWTN were the friars themselves, especially their Father Guardian, the late Fr. Angelus Shaughnessy, OFM Cap.,[25] who was "on loan" to the friary from a Capuchin

[25] Fr. Angelus died during the final days of preparing this manuscript. Turn to the appendix for a brief tribute to this wise and holy priest.

community in Pittsburgh. He was a seasoned priest who gave up a career in professional baseball to preach the gospel, living for many years with the very poorest of the poor in Papua New Guinea. Above all, he was a man of love. Here was a man who knew something about the power of a sacramental life.

In my early days as a Catholic, my inner world was wracked with sorrow. I remained distant from my wife. I struggled to love and serve my children in a divided home. My professional life was also in shambles: I had left the academic life and was trying, with little success, to make a career in the financial world. Finally, becoming Catholic had not instantly transformed my character. I battled dark places in my soul that drew me away from the ideals I was trying to embrace and to live.

For four years, I drove regularly to the friary to pour out my tears, my failings, and sometimes my self-pity. I confessed my sins. I confessed my sorrows. I shared my longing to be reconciled to my wife. Jill and I had reached some agreement about our children's education, but our emotional lives remained distant and cold. I wanted desperately to regain her love.

All the Franciscan priests were wonderful confessors, but Fr. Angelus had a special gift. He had a way of patiently drawing me to what mattered most. When I finished my confession, he would always ask, "Is there anything else?"

I didn't feel judged or condemned, but encouraged. Fr. Angelus made me feel as if he had all the time in the world to help plumb the depths of my soul and to bring healing.

One thing Fr. Angelus did for me was to validate my feelings of loss, mourning, and sorrow. He did not encourage me in self-pity, but neither did he dismiss the depth of my suffering. He helped shape my feelings about my wife, our marriage, and our children. He helped me separate the unhelpful feelings of guilt from the authentic feelings of loss or mourning that could lead me to a better state of mind and soul.

In a broken marriage, there is a temptation to hurt the other person, and a complementary temptation to carry around all the guilt, hurt, and pain that your spouse heaps on you. Sometimes, it feels as if the price of reconciliation is owning all that guilt and pain yourself. "I'm sorry, I'm sorry, I'm sorry, I'm sorry."

The confessional teaches you that there is a big difference between contrition and guilty feelings. Contrition is a recognition that I have done wrong and that I sincerely want to do better. If I bring my contrition to the confessional, the priest absolves me, I receive grace, and I go out encouraged. This is very different from guilt. Guilt is an emotion—and not necessarily a rational one. Guilt wants to bear the responsibility for the other's pain, to punish oneself, and sometimes to wallow in self-pity.

Guilt is also very different from mourning. Mourning is sorrow for an unrecoverable loss. When a loved one dies, we mourn because we will not see the person again in this life. Jesus said that this is an entirely reasonable emotion, even a virtuous one. "Blessed are those who mourn," He said (Matt. 5:4). Virtuous mourning does not leave you wallowing in self-pity or guilt, but instead it motivates you to make the most of your time and to be thankful for what you have.

In the confessional with Fr. Angelus, I learned to be contrite for my sins and to mourn the loss of my wife's affections, but my confessor saved me from guilt. I believe that this is essential for the healing of a marriage. Guilty spouses are like drowning victims, constantly climbing on top of each other and shoving each other under the waves. That has to end for the marriage to be healed.

Fr. Angelus did not make me "happy," at least not in the sense that I felt satisfied or content with my situation. Much more importantly, he made me sane. He straightened out my thinking about marriage, loss, guilt, and pain, and he gave me hope and a very long-term perspective. Through the confessional, I came to believe that in time, maybe a long time, and with grace, it would all work out.

Fr. Angelus did not counsel me all that much. His gift was not so much in what he said, but in who he was. He became for me the face of Christ, patiently forgiving and drawing me all the time back to what really mattered—away from myself, away from my self-pity, and toward a true assessment of my situation.

There are priests who mistake permissiveness for compassion, but Fr. Angelus was not one of them. The worst thing a priest can do is to devalue a man's confession and lead him astray by telling him that a real sin is not a sin. There are priests who say, "Well, now, we're only human. Perhaps the Church is wrong to ask this of you." If Fr. Angelus had done that, I might never have healed my marriage. Instead, he always pointed me patiently, lovingly, but consistently toward the goal: purity, fidelity, forgiveness, and reconciliation. With man, this is impossible; but all things are possible with God.

* * *

For four years, I lived as a Catholic without my wife's affections—but I never feared divorce. She was too committed to her children, and together we were striving to raise them well. What we lacked was emotional intimacy, warmth, and trust. Marriage felt like a desert. In these years, I began to appreciate more deeply the role of the Blessed Mother in the life of a Catholic man.

I learned about the saints from Scripture and Church history, and I was no longer afraid to ask them for their prayers. But the Blessed Virgin Mary is a special case.

The Blessed Virgin Mary is the subject of biblical prophecy in a unique way. In the book of Genesis, we learn of "the woman" whose seed will crush the head of the Serpent (see 3:15). In the book of Revelation, we read about a woman who confronts the serpent, the Devil. She is crowned with stars, clothed with the sun, and stands with the moon under her feet. She gives birth to the Christ child, and to all those who believe in the name of Jesus (see chapter 12).

In the Gospel of John, Jesus recognizes His mother, Mary, as "the woman." He answers her prayers at a wedding feast, even though His hour had not yet come (see John 2). On the Cross, He entrusts this "woman" to the apostle John and through him to the entire Church (John 19:26–27).

The "woman" of biblical prophecy is the antithesis (or antitype) of the first woman, Eve. The first woman disobeyed God but became the physical ancestor of the whole human race. The second woman, Mary, said yes to God and became the spiritual mother of all those who believe in Christ. She became the model Christian disciple, saying to the angel of the Annunciation, "Let it be to me according to your word" (Luke 1:38). It is no wonder the Church Fathers all hailed her as the second Eve. She is the only human creature whom the angels ever hailed and saluted as "full of grace" (Luke 1:28).

The Church tells us to hold all the saints in our hearts, to imitate their virtues, and to ask for their prayers and intercessions. But the Blessed Virgin Mary is a special case. She alone is our Mother in the faith. She alone is the perfect disciple. She alone is the Mother of God. She alone was commended directly to the Church by her divine Son.

When I first became Catholic, I had a hard time accepting and integrating into my spirituality all that the Church said about the Blessed Virgin. But I had promised to believe "everything which the Catholic Church declares to be revealed by God." Since the Church taught the Marian dogmas, I was determined to come to terms with them.

With help from Fr. Angelus, I began to turn more and more to the Virgin Mary in my heart and in my prayers. When we form a relationship with any of the saints, we take them to our heart and cherish their love and prayers. As I turned to the Blessed Virgin, though, I felt a special tenderness and care. Her absolute purity and chastity inspired me. Her humble acquiescence to the divine will challenged me. My confidence in her intercession emboldened me.

Through devotion to the Blessed Virgin, I was comforted with motherly and feminine affection even as I felt alienated from my wife. I entrusted Jill to her maternal care in the sincere hope that she would work on our marriage and one day bring us back together. It happened sooner than I thought possible. The Blessed Virgin Mary and once again St. Thérèse of Lisieux worked a miracle in my life.

* * *

Jill always loved France. When she was in ninth grade, a French teacher told her that she had no gift for languages and would never learn to speak French fluently. It was all that Jill needed to hear. Determined to prove that woman wrong, Jill began studying French obsessively and was fluent by the time she left high school.

Jill hosted French exchange students and even made several trips to the country. She fell in love especially with the south of France, where she made several good friends. The language and the culture also had a huge impact on our lives together: I met Jill in a French class, and in college we studied abroad in France and had a wonderful, romantic time. At the risk of sounding cliché, French was our special love language. For years, we called each other cute little French nicknames.

When Jill was barricaded indoors during the terrible Iowa winter, she taught my oldest son to speak French, and we ended up filling our house with French comics, children's books, movies, and music. We hosted French friends for dinner and conversation whenever we could.

When I became interested in the Catholic Church, therefore, it was easy to introduce French saints into our home. Even as Jill remained dead set against Catholicism, she read St. Thérèse's *Story of a Soul* enthusiastically and even gave copies to Protestant friends with her recommendation.

In 2007, Jill decided she wanted to take the family to France. My parents joined us and paid for the trip, as Jill and I were still finding our financial footing. Their generosity, we would come to see, was providential. We would go to Paris, the Loire Valley, and to Lisieux. And we would visit the home and the Basilica of St. Thérèse of Lisieux.

Much of the trip was a blur. We explored some lovely medieval churches, visited Versailles and the Chalets, and enjoyed French food. In Paris, we stopped by the Shrine of the Miraculous Medal on the Rue du Bac, the resting place of the relics of St. Catherine Labouré. But by far the most significant part of our trip was our visit to the Basilica of St. Thérèse.

When she stood before the relics of St. Thérèse, Jill uttered a silent prayer: "St. Thérèse, help us! Help our broken family. Help our broken marriage. Pray for us!" Jill said nothing to me about that prayer for many years. But the Little Flower answered that prayer. Enormous changes were just around the corner.

* * *

"Jill, would you go to Fr. Angelus for confession?"

"No."

"Please?"

"No. Don't ask again."

Once I discovered the miracle of Fr. Angelus Shaughnessy, I began pestering Jill to go back to confession. I don't know why, but I had a strong sense that if anyone could reach her for the Catholic Faith, it would be Fr. Angelus.

I do not remember when I started asking her to go; I only know that I was persistent. Meanwhile, the kids and I kept going to Mass on Sundays. Many weeks, Jill would stay home and watch television while the rest of us went to Mass. She had given up Christian worship almost entirely.

After months of pestering, Jill finally agreed to go see Fr. Angelus. It was clearly a concession to get me off her back. She had no interest in the sacrament for its own sake, but I didn't care: I promised to leave her alone if she would only go to see him once.

When she came home from that first meeting, I resisted the temptation to pepper her with questions about it. I left her alone about it and held my breath.

She went back the next week.

And the next week.

And the next week.

I didn't ask, and I certainly didn't complain.

After a few weeks of this, I was surprised in the middle of the night to wake up and find Jill missing from bed. I heard something in the dark, flipped on a light, and discovered Jill prostrate on the floor with a Rosary in her hand. She was praying the Rosary!

Shortly thereafter, I took a trip out of town for an investment seminar. I called home to check on Jill and the kids, and she told me, "I took the kids to daily Mass today, to vespers, to adoration of the Blessed Sacrament, and to Benediction." I was dumbfounded. Jill rarely attended Sunday Mass, and she certainly never attended a weekday Mass. I didn't know why, but Jill had begun to practice the Faith with enthusiasm.

It was clear to me that Jill was not doing this to humor me. After all, she was taking up devotions that I had never even practiced! Something happened to Jill in the confessional with Fr. Angelus, something that changed her life forever. But the real proof was not in her devotional life, but in what happened in her relationships.

Jill grew up in a chaotic home, filled with alcoholism, abandonment, and abuse. She had no examples of virtuous living. Her parents actively discouraged virtue. Her mother would say, "Quit studying. Put away your homework and come watch television!" Her mother would sit in front of daytime programs smoking, drinking, and cursing. Jill has memories of hiding under a neighbor's Christmas tree to escape a dangerous relative, and she witnessed fistfights break out over the coffin at a family funeral. And that's not even the worst of it.

As a result of this upbringing, Jill carried around a great deal of pain, broken relationships, and unforgiveness. So I knew that something amazing had happened in Jill's life when she began writing and calling her relatives. She offered apologies to all those she had hurt, and she asked for forgiveness. Perhaps even more challenging, she extended forgiveness to everyone who had ever hurt her. Some responded generously. Others were curt or dismissive. But it didn't matter. Jill was freeing herself from years of pain.

Most importantly, Jill extended forgiveness to those closer to home. She forgave my family for hurts she had carried around for years, and again she asked forgiveness for things she had done.

And she forgave me.

My wife forgave me for ten years of loss, pain, unfilled expectations, and broken promises. She forgave me for my studies, my selfishness, and my pride. She forgave me for my neglect, my immaturity, and my narcissism. She forgave me for my mistakes as a parent and for my professional failures. She forgave me for our relative poverty and lost opportunities. She forgave everything.

It was a long process. From her first confession with Fr. Angelus to Jill's total conversion, several months transpired. Jill dates her own conversion to January 22, 2008, six months from our visit to Lisieux. She went from no interest in the Catholic Faith to an overwhelming desire to give herself completely to Christ in the Church.

As always, Jill began to push ahead into areas I was afraid to look at; her reckless abandonment to divine providence carried us to the next phase of our marriage. She was prepared to rethink everything from the ground up.

I was very happy that Jill found Christ in the confessional. I was not happy with what she found out about our marriage.

Chapter 11

"Your Marriage Is Not Valid"

"Do you know what Fr. Bazzel told me?" Jill asked.

"What?"

"He told me that our marriage is not valid in the eyes of God or of the Church."

I was shocked and horrified. I did not see this coming.

"Whoa! Let's not jump to conclusions!" I answered.

In the fall of 2008, several months after Jill's re-conversion to the Faith, she approached a canon lawyer in our diocese, Fr. Kevin Bazzel, to ask him about the legal validity of our marriage. Why would she do such a thing? She told me later, "I didn't want anything to obstruct the flow of grace into my life. I wanted to do everything according to the Church. Nothing was more important to me."

For many people, the hardest part of the Church's teaching on marriage is the question of the validity of Christian marriage outside the Church. The reactions to a finding of invalidity are often harsh: "Who are you to tell me my marriage isn't valid? What can possibly be gained by telling people their marriage is not valid?"

I was one of those who did not want the Church passing judgment on my marriage. Things were finally starting to get better: I did not need some priest throwing the validity of my marriage into doubt. And so, again, I resisted.

Today, however, I am profoundly grateful for what Fr. Bazzel told my wife. It began the *real* healing of our marriage. Jill and I had both started to move closer to Christ in the confessional, but we started moving closer to *each other* because of a canon lawyer. It was not counseling or therapy that saved our marriage, but, incredibly, rules, regulations, and red tape.

* * *

Canon law—that is, the law of the Church—is the oldest continuous legal system in the Western world. It should not be surprising that the idea of marriage expressed in canon law would clash with modern notions. It turns out the difference is based in two fundamentally incompatible visions of married life.

The modern view of marriage is fundamentally about romantic love. We also generally understand marriage as a private, contractual relationship between two people that can be entered or exited more or less at will. This is very different from the traditional idea of marriage.

For most of human history, people did not marry for romantic love, but for economic and political reasons—to ensure legitimate offspring, to guarantee inheritance rights, and to form kinship bonds and alliances. Marriage was not a private affair at all, but a public institution that served the common good.

The Catholic Church accepts this ancient, public, and social conception of married life. Of course, the Church is not opposed to the idea of romantic love, but that kind of affection is not the *purpose* of marriage. From the Catholic point of view, you can have a perfectly successful marriage without romantic attraction.

After all, the ideal marriage is the marriage of Joseph and Mary, and they never had sexual relations. There is no indication that their relationship was characterized in any way by romantic attraction, certainly not in the modern understanding of that concept.

Now, there are also differences between the Catholic view of marriage and the views of other traditional societies. For instance, the Church teaches that Christian marriage serves not only civil society, but also the ecclesiastical community. Christian marriage is an ecclesial state, like being a monk, a nun, or a priest (CCC 1631). It exists not only for the good of the spouses, but for the good of the whole Christian community.

Christian marriage is also different because it is a sacrament—a symbol of a supernatural reality, a symbol through which God promises to bestow His grace on us. What is being symbolized in the Christian sacrament of marriage is not romantic love or even the perfect love of the Blessed Trinity, but the sacrificial love of Jesus Christ's suffering and death for the sake of His bride, the Church. Christ gave His life to bring His spouse to God.

Furthermore, the effect of the grace that is given through the sacrament of marriage is not to enable or to facilitate romantic love. God gives grace in the sacrament of marriage to enable the spouses to love sacrificially, to bear wrongs, to forgive offenses, to be chaste, to welcome and educate children, and perhaps even to die in the service of one's family.

When Fr. Bazzel told Jill that our marriage was not valid, it started us on an important process of reflection about the meaning of marriage—both our marriage and marriage generally. In the end, we had our marriage blessed by the Church, but we had to rethink our vows: Were we able to commit to what looked like a life of suffering just because it was the right thing to do? It turned out that we had to say yes to suffering before God took our suffering away. And we had to give up on romance before God rekindled our romance.

* * *

What does it even mean to say that a marriage is not "valid"? What on earth is "validity"?

In a broad sense, something is valid if it works, if it brings about its intended effect. Philosophers speak of an argument being valid if its conclusion follows logically from its premises. In law, a valid contract is one that is legally binding. The celebration of a sacrament can also be understood as valid or invalid. In Catholic theology, a valid sacrament brings about its intended effect. An invalid sacrament (which is really no sacrament at all) does not.

Marriages, therefore, can be valid or invalid. In a valid marriage, the parties really do incur the duties and obligations of marriage and accrue its benefits, privileges, and rights. An invalid marriage is not really a marriage at all. The moral rights, duties, and benefits of marriage do not flow from it, and civil law, if it is to be just, ought not say otherwise.

The idea of validity is implicit in contemporary debates about so-called gay marriage. One side imagines that marriage is simply a right extended by the state that can be applied to any two (three? four?) people who want social privileges attached to their romantic relationships. By contrast, the defenders of tradition hold that marriage is something intrinsically and necessarily connected to our nature created as male and female. The state can no more convey the right to marry to same-sex couples than it can square the circle. Marriage is not just any kind of union. It is the kind of union naturally fulfilled in the procreation of children.[26]

Many people hold the idea that they get to decide on their own whether they are validly married or not. The current civil

[26]Patrick Lee and Robert P. George, *Conjugal Union: What Marriage Is and Why It Matters* (Cambridge: Cambridge University Press, 2014), 47.

law on marriage exacerbates that tendency. If you want a marriage license, you fill out the paperwork. If you want a divorce, you file with the court. "No-fault" divorce is the law of land. Since the civil courts today default to the will of the parties, many people draw the false conclusion that nothing else matters but their own will in the matter.

New Catholics are often surprised to learn that the Church does not see it this way. Marriage is not simply a cultural construct that means whatever we want it to mean. It is not simply the desire for children or for intimacy that creates the conditions for marriage. Rather, marriage is something that derives from the natural law. When it comes to marriage, the Church does not arbitrarily create the conditions for validity. The conditions for a true and valid marriage flow from our nature created as male and female.[27]

The Church does not invent or impose those conditions. She merely recognizes them. It is not only to Catholics that She speaks, and it is not only about Christian marriage that She teaches. The Church has authority from Christ to judge all moral questions, including the validity of natural marriage.[28] The Church discerns and teaches those moral norms that emerge not only from revelation but also from natural law.[29]

The case is a bit different with respect to Christian marriage. Christian marriage presupposes the conditions for a valid, natural marriage, i.e., one man and one woman united indissolubly for life

[27]"The personal bond of marriage is established precisely at the natural level of the male or female mode of being a human person." Pope St. John Paul II, "God Himself Is the Author of Marriage," *L'Osservatore Romano*, English ed., February 7, 2001, 3, posted at EWTN, https://www.ewtn.com/library/PAPALDOC/JP2MATR.HTM.

[28] See *Code of Canon Law* 747.2; *Veritatis Splendor*, no. 110.

[29] *Humanae Vitae*, no. 4.

for the good of the spouses and the bearing and raising of offspring. But Christian marriage is also an ecclesial state. It grants certain rights and privileges within the Church. Furthermore, when both spouses are baptized Christians and at least one of them is Catholic, they need to associate their marriage with the sacramental life of the Church. The Mass, the Eucharist, and Confession are essential to living a fruitful, grace-filled Catholic marriage. For these reasons, it makes good sense for the Church to want Her children to marry in a sacred ceremony, closely allied to the Church and Her sacraments.

In view of these considerations, canon law obligates Catholics to marry in a Catholic Church before an ordained Catholic minister—a priest or a deacon. This is true even if one party is unbaptized and the marriage is not sacramental. Failure to do so renders the marriage invalid.

There are several potential impediments to marriage in Church law: In our case, what mattered was the question of Jill's Catholic identity at the time of our marriage. She had been baptized and confirmed in the Catholic Church, and so, for purposes of canon law, she was a Catholic, even though she had ceased practicing the Faith after confirmation. Unfortunately, we married outside the Church before a Protestant minister. Therefore, our marriage was invalid. (Had the Church considered Jill to be Protestant, rather than Catholic, we would have been exempt from the requirement to marry before an ordained Catholic minister, and we could still have contracted a valid and sacramental marriage.)

It is important to be precise: To say that a sacrament is invalid *does not mean* that the persons involved have been denied all grace. God can always extend grace if He chooses. In fact, the prompting and nudging toward faith or holiness that Catholics call *actual grace* routinely occurs outside the sacraments, as Christ draws people to receive the grace of baptism. (Baptized people also receive actual graces.) But the habitual grace made available through the Christian sacrament of marriage cannot be presumed apart from a valid sacrament. An invalid marriage cannot give rise to sacramental grace.

I can say with certainty that my conscience was clear at the time of my wedding. I was not a Catholic at the time and had no intention of becoming one, and so I had no regard for the requirements of Church law. Jill also was clear in her conscience, though she didn't understand her canonical obligations. She had ceased to believe in the Catholic Church and felt no obligation to the Church's law. Both of us intended to contract a Christian marriage as we understood the institution at that time. We sought God's grace and commended ourselves to His mercy. We prayed that He would bless our union.

But even if we may have been innocent at the time of our wedding, we stopped being innocent the moment we learned of our canonical obligation. At that point, we had a moral obligation to resolve the discrepancy. God might have sent us actual grace in our *ignorance*. It would be presumption to assume He would overlook *disobedience*.

* * *

Today, I more fully appreciate these fine distinctions. Grace, validity, obligation, and conscience are related in complex ways, but at the time the nuances were lost on me. "Your marriage is not valid" had a pretty stark ring to it, and it threw me into another crisis of conscience.

I was worried that this new challenge might introduce new tensions that could sabotage the progress we had made in warmth and intimacy over the past several months. Deep down inside, however, I was worried about something else. I knew that, in reality, resolving the problem was a simple matter. All we had to do was repeat our marriage vows in the presence of a priest; it would hardly take an hour of our life. But it was more than that: I would have to stand in the presence of a priest and reaffirm my marriage to Jill without reservation. I didn't want to admit it to myself, but this is what bothered me the most: I really was not sure I wanted to restate those marriage vows.

Just about the only reason I had persevered for those ten years was the promise I made to be faithful. Was that promise invalid? Did that mean my suffering and sacrifice all those years were worthless? (No, it did not mean that, as I would learn later.) What nearly drove me to madness was the idea that I had an out that I could have taken. Did I now want to close that door forever?

Oddly, a priest affirmed this apprehension. I opened up about my feelings in the confessional one afternoon at the parish.

"I've been told I might need to have my marriage convalidated," I said to him.

"You know if you do this," he said, "you'll have no chance of ever getting an annulment."

I thought it was strange counsel to give a suffering penitent. Did he really want to encourage me to leave my family? It turned out, however, it was the best thing he could have said to me. The stark choice he presented was the beginning of another radical change in my life.

My options were clear. On one hand, there was a way out of my pain: If my marriage wasn't valid, then I didn't have to stay.

On the other hand, I could restate my vows and lock myself in forever. What would it mean to promise lifelong fidelity where I didn't feel love? Years later, I would learn that Jill was experiencing the exact same struggle. Our feeling of love for one another had faded almost to nothing over those hard years. Did we want to pledge ourselves to one another once again?

We both wrestled with the essence of marriage. Is it a romantic union defined by affection? Or does one promise fidelity for some other reason, such as the welfare of children?

The stark realism of this choice was the best thing that ever happened to our marriage. Both of us decided to restate our marriage vows for the sake of our children. Years later, I asked Jill, "Why did you do it? Why did you decide to convalidate our marriage?"

You must understand that Jill and I love each other very, very deeply today. Neither one of us regrets our marriage. We would both do it all again in a heartbeat. But that is not what we felt at the time.

Jill replied, "I did it in order to suffer. I consciously chose suffering because it was the right thing to do."

It was the beginning of the deepest love either of us had ever known.

Chapter 12

Treasure in a Field

> By the very fact, therefore, that the faithful with sincere mind give such consent, they open up for themselves a treasure of sacramental grace from which they draw supernatural power for the fulfilling of their rights and duties faithfully, holily, perseveringly even unto death.[30]

We restated our wedding vows before a Catholic priest on December 12, 2007. Now we were certain that ours was a valid, sacramental Catholic marriage. We were not naïve about what that meant: Yes, God would give us grace, but, no, He would not make it easy. Expecting nothing but hardship, neither of us was prepared for what came next.

In the months that followed the convalidation of our marriage, my wife began to glow, and she hasn't stopped glowing since. She gave me her heart and has never taken it back. As for me, it was impossible for me not to fall head over heels in love with this woman again. Those who have known us the longest testify to the miracle

[30]Pius XI, encyclical *Casti Connubii* (On Christian Marriage) (December 31, 1930), no. 40.

that took place in our lives. I called a friend one day to report, "I'm in marital bliss." "I know," he replied. "Everything has changed. It's impossible not to notice."

Sacraments are not magic; they don't change your life just because you say certain words or participate in certain religious rites. The sacraments represent truths about the moral and spiritual life, and they guarantee divine assistance—but only if you sincerely commit to living out those truths. If you approach the sacraments without that disposition—without faith and charity—the grace of the sacrament is inert, unused, and unprofitable. It is like a treasure buried in a field.

The grace of the sacrament of marriage began to work in our lives because we accepted the truth that was represented in the sacrament, and then we committed to living that truth as vigorously as possible. The truth of Christian marriage is that husbands and wives are to lay down their lives for one another to bring their spouse and their children to God. That "laying down one's life" entails the willing embrace of suffering—even at the hands of one's family—trusting that God will redeem that suffering.

"Laying down one's life" does not mean taking up the role of the wounded victim in order to manipulate others. The truth of the sacrament means laying down our masks and giving up all posturing and posing. We mustn't play the righteous warrior, the spiritually enlightened, the innocent bystander, or any other stance meant to justify or to manipulate. Instead, we must commit to living in the truth about ourselves—both the beautiful and the ugly.

To lay down one's life authentically means sacrificing our plans, our priorities, and our goals for God's plans, priorities, and goals. God's plan is that through marriage I, my wife, and my children, can come to live faith-filled, virtuous lives and, in turn, can be a source of blessing to those around us. Everything else—talents, career, physical health and safety, education—must be subordinate to that goal.

For the grace of the sacrament to begin to flow, Jill and I both had to die to certain habits and dispositions. But even though both of us had to change our lives and our attitudes about marriage, we each did so in different ways. I had to accept that marriage is not a platform from which to live out my professional aspirations, nor a place to recreate those aspirations in my children. Marriage is not about gratifying my appetites or palliating my emotional wounds. For her part, Jill had to accept that marriage is not a hermetically sealed bubble immune from suffering. Marriage is a service and a gift we give to one another, to our children, and to society.

It is not easy to make changes like that. It takes time, patience, self-examination, brutal honesty, admitting wrong, and sincere attempts to do better—and, of course, a lot of grace. That is why Christ gave us the whole sacramental system, especially the sacrament of confession. It was in the confessional that God unraveled the knots in our lives so that grace could begin to flow.

* * *

In college, Jill and I studied the French wars of religion. We were sympathetic to the plight of the suffering Huguenots—French Protestants—and followed their footsteps when we traveled to Europe, visiting the city of Aigues-Mortes and the Tower of Constance, where Huguenot prisoners were held. Jill was particularly moved by the life of prisoner Marie Durand, a laywoman imprisoned from 1730 to 1768. The curator pointed out to us the words she had scrawled in the stone beneath our feet: "Resist!"

Like many people who have suffered childhood trauma, Jill had become hyper alert to possible threats. Like Marie Durand, she planted her feet and took a defensive stance toward the world. In the early years of our marriage, as we grew further and further apart,

Jill's stance toward me also became defensive. I hurt her, and she was not going to let herself be hurt again. She walled herself up against me as surely as Marie Durand was walled up in Aigues-Mortes.

There was no way through her defenses. How can you recover from complete emotional withdrawal? Years later, I asked Jill, "What did Fr. Angelus say to you? How did he reach you when no one else could?"

"He told me that my suffering had meaning. He told me that my suffering was not worthless or wasted. No one had ever told me that before."

It is risky to tell another person that his suffering is meaningful because it feels presumptuous, but Fr. Angelus had earned the right to say it. He could speak into Jill's life in a way no one else could. Fr. Angelus told me one time that he prayed God would strike him dead if he ever lost patience in the confessional. He had that God-given gift.

We are all going to suffer. There's no avoiding it. You can resist all you like, but you cannot prevent all suffering. The secret to Catholic spirituality is realizing that God brings good out of evil, and that even suffering has a purpose. God rewards those who suffer with faith and trust in His goodness.

Jill became willing to embrace suffering. When she pronounced her vows at our convalidation, Jill understood that she was accepting the possibility, and more likely the probability, of marital suffering. She took the risk of opening herself to me. She put down her defenses and, in so doing, opened herself up to grace.

* * *

I am the younger of two sons. As a small child, I regarded my parents and my older brother with a certain degree of awe. My parents were both successful professionals—my father an attorney and my mother a college instructor. My brother was always an outstanding storyteller, an artist, and a designer, and today he is an award-winning publisher, art designer, and writer. I felt as if my family members all had talents well beyond what I could hope for. What I remember most acutely from childhood was a deep sense of inadequacy. Next to my parents' professionalism and my brother's artistic talents, I felt like a nonentity.

As I grew older, I nurtured my self-pity by withdrawing. I spent less time with my family and finally went to boarding school in ninth grade. By the time I met Jill, I had been brooding more or less alone for years. I did not have a strong sense of a coherent family life rooted in the virtues. Instead, I envied professional competence as the mark of success. And so, when I finally began to take command of my own destiny, personal ambition motivated me far more than truth or charity. Perhaps surprisingly (and naïvely), I began my studies seeing theology more as a path to professional success than a reflection on the wisdom of tradition.

Authentic Catholic faith and the sacrament of marriage destroyed my early professional ambition. I had wanted to be a college or seminary professor, and I had wanted to live vicariously through my children, whom I would raise as little prodigies. By 2008, those aspirations lay in ruins. There was no chance I would ever hold a tenured position at a university, and I learned that my kids are wonderful but very different from me. We each have our own interests and talents.

As I thought through the Church's teaching on marriage and family, I realized how impoverished my priorities were and how poorly equipped I was to live well. I had to offer my children more than academic formation and religious indoctrination; I had to offer them guidance in developing virtue. To do that, I needed more than intellectual understanding of the virtues: I needed to possess them. I would have to possess and to model empathy, compassion, fortitude, justice, prudence, temperance, and a whole host of attributes I was lacking.

My confessors never chastised me for making too little money or failing to make tenure. Instead, they pointed me to the Cross, by emphasizing small, measurable, daily habits of virtue. Another priest who had a profound influence on my life is my friend and mentor Fr. Lambert Greenan, O.P. Fr. Lambert told me over and over about his own father, who was not wealthy but never failed in his daily prayers, always took the family to the sacraments, and never raised his voice—but he did insist on the loving discipline of a well-regulated home.

When I yielded to the sacrament of marriage, I had to accept a completely different sense of myself and my needs, goals, and aspirations. I recognized that I was indeed inadequate, but it was not professional competence I lacked. What I needed were the virtues. I had to let go of my old goals—but they were dead anyway, so what did I have to lose? I turned instead to a new ambition: How could I learn to be a virtuous father and build character in my children, regardless of their professional aspirations?

* * *

In his 1930 encyclical on Christian marriage, *Casti Connubii*, Pope Pius XI explained that many people do not benefit from the grace of the sacrament of matrimony because they do not cooperate with it:

> Nevertheless, since it is a law of divine Providence in the supernatural order that men do not reap the full fruit of the Sacraments which they receive after acquiring the use of reason unless they cooperate with grace, the grace of matrimony will remain for the most part an unused talent hidden in the field unless the parties exercise these supernatural

> powers and cultivate and develop the seeds of grace they have received. (no. 41)

In two places, Jesus compares the grace of Christian life to a treasure hidden in a field. In Matthew's Gospel, Jesus says that "the kingdom of heaven is like treasure hidden in a field, which a man found and covered up; then in his joy he goes and sells all that he has and buys that field" (13:44). And then a few chapters later, Jesus tells a parable about a master who gave each of his servants a sum of money to invest. Some put the money to good use, earning more money with what they had been given, but one simply buries his talent in a field. The master punishes this servant, taking away his talent and giving it to another (25:14–30).

Pope Pius compared the grace of matrimony to this treasure in a field. It is a tremendous gift, but to access this gift we must sell everything, so to speak. We must be willing to dig down into our lives and root out the impediments to grace—and the whole sacramental system of the Church facilitates this process. We confess our sins, do penance, and commit to amending our lives. We throw ourselves into the sacrifice of the Mass in imitation of Christ. We do everything in our power to cooperate with grace. And then, once we have received the beautiful gift of grace, we must live boldly, not burying it again out of fear.

Pope St. John Paul II wrote more on the topic of cooperation with grace in marriage than any pope in history. His letter *Familiaris Consortio* offers an extended catechesis on the pastoral care in marriage. One passage beautifully describes the life of a couple cooperating with God's grace in the sacrament of matrimony:

> There is no doubt that these conditions [necessary for living Christian married life] must include persistence and patience, humility and strength of mind, filial trust in God and in His grace, and frequent recourse to prayer and to the

> sacraments of the Eucharist and of Reconciliation. Thus strengthened, Christian husbands and wives will be able to keep alive their awareness of the unique influence that the grace of the sacrament of marriage has on every aspect of married life.[31]

After our convalidation, I became aware "of the unique influence that the grace of the sacrament of matrimony has on every aspect of married life." And I also began to see how grace was changing my wife, making her into a new mother and a new spouse. It filled me with gratitude to God and appreciation for the new virtues flowing into her life.

I also began to love and enjoy the faith that Jill and I shared much more completely. Our "recourse to prayer and the sacraments" stopped being something we fought about and became a regular aspect of life. I could turn to the sacraments not only in mourning and sorrow, but in celebration and joy. I felt hope flowing into my life for the first time in years.

Jill and I began to cooperate, perhaps for the first time ever, in a common vision of Christian family life. Until January 2008, Jill and I had never really shared the same vision. We began our marital life thinking we had a Christian marriage, but we had very different ideas about what that would mean.

Initially, I thought my Christian vocation was as a teacher. Jill thought we should be missionaries. I wanted to delay children until I was ready professionally. Jill wanted children much sooner, in part to palliate her loneliness. I wanted to prepare my children academically. She wanted to protect them from harm. I thought I could be saved by "faith alone." Jill and I both felt a deep need for more than "faith alone." Both of us fought like mad to insulate

[31]John Paul II, apostolic exhortation *Familiaris Consortio* (November 22, 1981), no. 33.

ourselves from suffering. Both of us guaranteed we would inflict plenty of it on each other.

Through our slow growth into the Catholic Faith, Jill and I both acquired a completely different view of the vocation of marriage and the role of faith, virtue, and the sacraments in living out that vocation. There is a passage on Christian marriage in *Gaudium et Spes* from the Second Vatican Council that describes this new vision very well:

> Authentic married love is caught up into divine love and is governed and enriched by Christ's redeeming power and the saving activity of the Church, so that this love may lead the spouses to God with powerful effect and may aid and strengthen them in sublime office of being a father or a mother. For this reason Christian spouses have a special sacrament by which they are fortified and receive a kind of consecration in the duties and dignity of their state. By virtue of this sacrament, as spouses fulfil their conjugal and family obligation, they are penetrated with the spirit of Christ, which suffuses their whole lives with faith, hope and charity. Thus they increasingly advance the perfection of their own personalities, as well as their mutual sanctification, and hence contribute jointly to the glory of God.[32]

We could love and forgive each other everything. We could love our children. We could seek God together. Our shared work would be to raise our children in the true knowledge of God, which means the knowledge of faith, love, and virtue. In this way, and in no other, we could fulfill our vocation as a Christian married couple.

[32]Second Vatican Council, Pastoral Constitution on the Church in the Modern World *Gaudium et Spes* (December 7, 1965), no. 48.

* * *

Grace does not destroy our nature and re-create us as something completely new. Rather, grace perfects our nature and elevates it to something supernatural. The Second Vatican Council speaks of "the perfection of their own personalities" that spouses can expect from the sacrament of marriage. When we said yes to God's grace in the sacrament, gave up our previous plans, accepted the probability of suffering, reoriented our priorities around a new understanding of marriage, and turned with purpose to the practice of a sacramental life and to prayer, God began to perfect, or at least to improve, our personalities.

The easiest way to convey the change in our lives is to turn to my wife's diary. A month after our convalidation, something began to happen in Jill's heart. She shared nothing of this with me at the time, but she did pour it out on the page.

One month after the convalidation, January 22, 2008, Jill wrote the following:

> "As much as we love the person we love the least, that is how much we love Jesus."
>
> —Fr. Angelus Shaughnessy, OFM Cap.

Then, I found these prayers in Jill's own words:

> Lord, give me love for those I do not love.
>
> Jesus, grant me love for those I am tempted not to love so that I will be worthy of Your love.
>
> My Lord, I thank You for the humiliation of the flesh [so] that I long to take refuge in You and You alone.
>
> Thank You for reminding me of my unworthiness that I not take You for granted.

> Thank You for the thanklessness and misunderstanding of men.
>
> I am so, so, so sorry for my ingratitude.
>
> Thank You for letting me be of service to You in any way, since I know You don't need me at all. Thank You for this precious gift, for it gives me joy and draws me close to You.
>
> I shall never complain again.... Last night God graced me with the presence of His mother.... For that time, I was truly able to see what it is like to love my enemies with equal or greater love than the love I have for those I love most. I tried it out by reflecting on all I dislike, and I couldn't but love them deeply.

Not long after that, Jill wrote a letter to the priests of the Birmingham Diocese in which she explained what happened:

> I went from believing nothing with great zeal to believing everything the Church said. In a moment, I received infused love of God and the Church and was completely transformed.... I had an intense desire for the sacraments. I went to confession to Fr. Anthony many times. I then went to Mass. Fr. Anthony preached on how the love of God should make our hearts change for good and He should be our All in All. I felt as though he was talking to me.... My longing to receive the Eucharist was so intense.

In Japanese culture, and especially on the island of Okinawa, there is a concept called ikigai. Roughly, it means "reason for being," or "reason for getting up in the morning," and incorporates the idea of orienting one's whole life around a calling. I have no doubt that Jill took up a new ikigai on that day.

Reading forward to January 24, I found this:

> Reading to the children tonight, I realized that the goal of life is to find Jesus, and having found Him, to serve Him.

For Jill, this meant forgiving everyone, loving her enemies as much as she loved her friends, and gratefully accepting whatever suffering came her way in imitation of Christ. It didn't resolve all her problems, and it certainly didn't end all her suffering. It didn't prevent her from making mistakes, from offending people, or from getting frustrated. But inside, Jill began to radiate the light of Christ. Once, there had been an emotional vacuum—deep wounds from years of suffering and neglect, protected by hardened layers. Now there was an openness to the world, to others, to experience, and to God.

* * *

I did not keep a diary like Jill, but I can distinctly remember some of the important spiritual changes that took place in my life at that time. I certainly did not suddenly become virtuous. Apart from some extraordinary act of God, we cannot acquire virtues without practice. What changed is that I began *to aim for virtue* in a new way—especially the virtue of prudence.

Prudence is the virtue of good decision-making. Unlike academic skill, we cannot acquire prudence simply by mastering theories and facts. We learn prudence, rather, by spending time with prudent people, both here with us and in history, and by paying careful attention to their decisions and seeking to imitate them. We ask questions, take counsel, test, and retest. I began to seek out good Catholic fathers in my diocese, both spiritual (priests) and natural, to ask them how they did it. How did they keep their kids off drugs, or keep them chaste, or encourage prayerfulness, responsibility, and selflessness? I might have known more than most about the history of theology, but I had to accept that I knew precious little about being a good Catholic father.

The other thing I had to learn was to die over, and over, and over again to my professional aspirations, my disappointments, my anxieties, and my unhealthy attachments. In graduate school, I had become so anxious about my work that I induced severe, lasting, and debilitating panic attacks. The prospect of failure filled me with so much terror that some days I could barely rise from bed. One thing that helped me recover is what the Church calls mental prayer. This is not the prayer of petition, in which we ask God for good things, but instead a lengthy meditation upon some truth of the Faith, allowing it to work upon the mind, imagination, and emotions. When I determined to reform my life, I retired each day for twenty, thirty, or even sixty minutes in order to give myself to this type of meditation. I would reflect on the immensity of God, more present to me than I am to myself. I would contemplate the sacrament of matrimony, and through it my participation in the mystery of Christ's suffering. And sometimes I would adore Christ in the Blessed Sacrament, a privileged form of devotion.

I do not claim that I have been cured of all that ails my soul, but this much is true: The depression slowly lifted; the anxiety receded; and my wife began to notice the change in my outlook and disposition. She was never very proud of my academic success; in fact, she resented it. But now she began to express pride *in my fatherhood*. She thanked me for what I did for her, for the kids, and the family. I felt a deeper, more satisfying fulfillment than what I ever expected or could have received from professional life. I felt new meaning in my life, a transcendence born amidst the mundane world of Legos, carpools, and dirty diapers.

Everything changed for us in January 2008. Two months later, Jill turned to me and said, "David, we should have another child." And I agreed.

We conceived our fifth child, the child of our conversion, the child of our Catholic faith.

Chapter 13

Parenthood

One of the most important aspects of our journey to the Catholic Church was the way it was driven by and, in turn, reformed our view of parenting. Jill and I sought grace in the sacraments so that we could be good parents. We accepted suffering so that we could be good parents. We finally came together in a common vision of family life so that we could be good parents. We fell in love with one another again because we wanted to be good parents.

We experienced many setbacks, failures, and disappointments as parents. We saw our children suffer from our errors, and we strove to understand why. We sought counsel, read books, and consulted priests and other mentors. We pored over our past faults, looked at our present lives, and thought about where we needed to go. The fruit of that reflection was a thorough embrace of the Catholic Faith and, ultimately, the healing of our marriage.

The Church tells us that families should be life-affirming communities, working together to serve society and the Church. Families are not just boarding houses of autonomous individuals pursuing private pleasures. When we first had children, neither one of us really understood that. Each of us had grown up with a lot of autonomy and loneliness, and so we had found solace in private pursuits.

Naturally, we wanted to share our interests with our children. We lacked, however, a common vision of a purposeful family life.

I wanted to have little academic or musical prodigies. Jill just wanted to protect her children from the pains she had suffered. We both wanted our children to be Christians and to go to Heaven, but we had a very weak conception of what Christian life actually entailed. These earliest goals were not enough to make us good parents. Academic excellence and musical skill are not enough if they are not combined with justice and charity. A life sheltered from suffering will not prepare you to sacrifice for others. You cannot raise children who serve society and the Church if they lack virtue.

I now see that children need virtues more than information or talent. They need to value transcendence more than "success." Heroism and imagination inspire them more than lectures on right and wrong. They need to risk failure and injury, and not just be sheltered from harm. And parents cannot give what they do not have. Parents need to become virtuous, honorable, informed, and engaged. Kids value what you do far more than what you say. And they need a home secured by the unconditional love of parents for one another.

That is not who we were when we got married. Jill and I were morally weak, unimaginative, and wounded people who clung to our narrow views and our private goals. It was inevitable that our family would suffer from our parental myopia. By God's grace, loss and disappointment drove us to consider what went wrong and to find healing in the Catholic Church.

* * *

"I'm pregnant."

It was September in 1994. Jill and I were in our small, upstairs apartment in Highwood, Illinois. I was one year away from finishing my seminary degree at Trinity Evangelical Divinity School. I looked at those two lines on the pregnancy test and felt like the whole world ended and was re-created in an instant. It was a new universe, one containing my child. Everything was different now.

"Jill, you know what this means?" I asked. "It means we have to be perfect."

I was thrilled and terrified, overcome by a profound sense of moral obligation. I needed to be perfect for my child—to give my child the best possible life, to offer him the opportunities I wish I had, and to prevent the mistakes I regretted. I ached with longing, feeling as if I had myself been re-created in this tiny person. I burst into tears and laughter when Jonathan was finally born. I thanked God for this miracle.

At the time, though, I had poorly formed thoughts on parenthood. I knew what I wanted for my child—happiness, success, talent, learning, and religious faith—but I had little notion of how to achieve these things. And, at the very root of things, I had almost no thoughts about why I should have children at all. It just seemed like "what you do."

Why would I want to have children? What are children for? I do not think I ever asked myself these questions. I suppose I just wanted friendship from my children—not the kind of friendship shared with peers, but a loving, mutual, and satisfying relationship that could last for life. I think I also wanted to live vicariously through my offspring: I failed to reach many of my childhood goals, and so I hoped my children could do better. Finally, I hoped for some form of redemption through parenthood. Would parenthood give me an opportunity to correct the mistakes I had made in my own life?

It was very clear, on the other hand, why Jill wanted children: She was lonely and wanted love. She longed to have an innocent, uncorrupted soul on whom to pour out her affection. She had loved before and been rejected, but her child, she was sure, would not reject her. She told me once, "If I just love them, they will love me back."

There is nothing wrong with wanting your children to love you. There is nothing wrong with wanting them to be successful and with taking pride in their accomplishments. But these were not sufficient reasons to have children.

Jill and I now understand that parenthood is a sacred duty and a privilege, not an entitlement. We have children for the good of the family, society, and the Church, not to palliate the emotional wounds of their parents. We succeed or fail as parents not when children master the skills or talents we value, but when they flourish as virtuous, compassionate people who serve the common good. Friendship and sharing and redemption can happen, but these are happy side effects, not the goal, of good parenting.

For a Catholic, the ultimate parenting examples are Mary and Joseph. Did Mary become a parent to palliate her own emotional wounds, to make friends, or to make up for past mistakes? Did Joseph accept becoming foster father to Jesus for these reasons? On the contrary, an angel appeared to each of them announcing a birth that would pierce their own souls with tragic sorrow, but that would also save God's people from their sins. How did the Holy Couple respond to this announcement? "Be it done to me according to thy word!"

The first several years of parenthood were years of acrimonious conflict in our marriage. I was not wrong when I said that parenthood demands perfection, but Jill and I had very different views on what perfection meant. It was only in the Catholic Faith that we found a unified and unifying vision of what family life was and could be. Only after our turn to the Faith and several years of sacramental life were Jill and I able to reform our marriage and our understanding of parenthood. Today, our commitment to Catholic parenting is a source of strength, unity, love, and purpose.

* * *

Jonathan came home from the hospital at the end of May in 1995. I placed him in his crib, in which I had hung a Fischer-Price tape recorder on which I played Vivaldi for my tiny infant, hoping to start him out on a life of music. I had big plans: Suzuki violin at age three, then French, Latin, and Greek as soon as possible. I often held baby Jonathan in my arms while scanning my bookshelf, pointing out the authors I liked. And of course, I read to him as often as I could. He was going to become everything I hoped to be: smart, talented, articulate, and focused.

For Jill it was different. Her childhood was marked by insecurity and instability, and so it made sense that her orientation as a parent was more toward protection.

My childhood sorrows were more from a sense of inadequacy than one of insecurity. I felt like a failure in comparison with my older and more talented brother, and I never could compete with other boys in sports. What I wanted for my son was not safety but competence. I'd give him skills and talents to make his way in the world. He'd be a success. He would be *significant*.

Each of us parented out of our insecurities and fears and, lacking any common vision, we had no clear way to integrate our concerns. The deeper we entered parenthood, the more our emotions came into conflict.

* * *

Jill and I did do some good things as a team in those first years as parents. We both agreed on the value of foreign languages, and we worked hard to teach our children French. The language became something our kids could take pride in, a common interest that united our family.

We also introduced our two oldest sons to chess, and they took quickly to the game and advanced rapidly. In a few years, they began to compete in state tournaments, sometimes placing first or second in the state for their age groups. Unlike other aspects of my children's upbringing, I didn't get behind chess because it gratified some unfulfilled childhood longing: I supported my boys' chess career simply because it was good.

Chess is the kind of practice that builds virtue. The boys could not advance without hard work, concentration, practice, and focus. They learned to delay gratification and to set long-term goals, and in turn they both grew in confidence. Chess became another thing our family could unite around. We took trips out of town to compete in tournaments and made a lot of friends along the way.

The Catholic Church teaches that goodness is diffusive, which means that goodness tends to multiply itself. If you start a good thing or simply put virtue into daily practice, something else good is more likely to happen. We saw this with chess. One of the Dominican sisters at the boys' school began a chess club in school just for my son Jonathan. His interest in chess had a ripple effect on others around him.

We also learned that there is a patron saint of chess players, St. Teresa of Avila, the great Carmelite contemplative. One of the Dominican sisters was friends with a Carmelite nun, who began praying for Jonathan and the chess club. This turned out, as we will see, to be incredibly important for the healing of my marriage.

When I look back over our years of parenting, these are the kinds of things I really value. The best moments were when we shared each other's joys and triumphs and grew in virtue striving after common goals. Mastering chess and French were such goals we could all get behind. Through these things, my kids grew in virtue and independence, and their growth had an exponential effect on those around them.

The Church tells us that families should be life-affirming communities, working together to serve society and the Church, and that what serves that common vision is good for family life. The way to build life-affirming communities is to center them on practices that serve the common good. It doesn't have to be chess: It could be any consistent, rule-governed activity that requires some form of cooperation and virtue. When such a thing is done for the love of God, it is even more beautiful.

We tried to teach our kids the Faith in several ways, but I think we were most successful when we worked together for a common goal. The whole family supported the local pro-life ministry with volunteer time, donations, and prayers. Jill often took the children to visit the sick and the aged. We opened our home in hospitality to friends and strangers. We often spoke about social, ethical, theological, and moral issues. But we had the greatest difficulty in what you might call "formal catechesis," including maintaining a common prayer or devotional life.

* * *

It took me a long time to figure out what I was doing right and wrong in parenting.

It helped me to think a lot about my own parents and grandparents. My paternal grandfather was not a Catholic, but he was a man of great integrity. At his funeral, strangers approached to tell us how much he had meant to them. I once asked my uncle, "What did Granddad do in his spare time?" My uncle said, "He didn't have any spare time. He worked all the time to support his family." He was a far better man than I will ever be.

My grandfather was a Baptist, and I suspect he would have been rather horrified to learn I have become a Catholic. His life, however, has taught me a lot about the Catholic Faith. As a good Baptist, he believed in "faith alone" and "Scripture alone"—but what made him a great man and a great father was not actually faith alone—and certainly not how that is conceived by Protestants.

He was great because of his habits of virtue. In a sense, his family and his culture taught him better than his religion did.

My grandfather was the first in his family to go to college, but he graduated during the Depression. He worked all night during school to pay his tuition and ended up being the only member of his graduating class to find a job. Eventually, he went into the car-rental business, building up a fleet of automobiles in Tuscaloosa, Alabama.

Granddad caught an employee stealing from him one day. He could have fired him on the spot, but instead he admonished him: "I know you better than that. That's not the kind of person you are." My grandfather's fairness and clemency won the man over; he went on to become one of the company's most faithful employees.

My dad worked alongside his father in the family business, but he didn't much enjoy it. Even so, I never heard my dad complain about this part of his life because at his father's side my dad learned important skills that served him for the rest of his life. The virtues he learned from his father were more important even than law school in making him into a successful and respected attorney.

There was one thing about Granddad that my father deeply resented, however: his constant and often angry lectures. My grandfather's favorite topic was the evils of alcohol, about which he would regularly dress down his sons.

As much as the boys hated his lectures, they revered their father. My grandfather had a powerful influence on them: They learned honesty, industry, and integrity from working alongside him. All of them ended up becoming successful professionals and entrepreneurs, and they are all practicing Christians in stable, long-lasting marriages. And every one of them drinks alcohol.

* * *

As I worked to understand my failures as a parent, I asked for counsel from many people, and I read a lot of books. Fr. Anthony Mary,

MFVA, who is a member of the order of Franciscan friars established by EWTN's Mother Angelica, once recommended that I read the works of James Stenson, who was a school headmaster for many years and made a personal study of successful kids and their parents. Stenson explained it all to me, and my failures as a parent made sense after that.

Stenson argues that the children of entrepreneurs do better than the children of professionals. What the successful families shared, he found, was a sense of mission and adventure—of shared purposeful activity that builds habits of virtue from the ground up. The children of entrepreneurs were more likely to do well because they were more likely to work with their parents in just such a common enterprise. Families without that sense of mission and with a more consumerist understanding of family life did less well.

Canadian psychologist Gordon Neufeld has argued something similar. Since World War II and the rise of professionalism in our economy, parents and children have grown apart. In traditional societies, adults are responsible for bringing children to maturity, but in our culture today it is increasingly children who bring their peers to maturity. Moreover, adult and youth culture are pitted against each other. Popular media such as *The Hunger Games* or *Divergent* depict youth and adults at war. Neufeld argues that parents must hold on to their kids because the outcomes for children raised by peers and youth culture are far worse.

When I read these things, I was amazed. My grandfather's life, my father's life, and my life suddenly made much more sense. I realized that my upbringing almost perfectly mirrored the social dynamics described by Stenson and Neufeld. My father grew up in a mission-driven, entrepreneurial family, where he learned virtue, but he *didn't realize* he was learning virtue. As a young man, my father grew to resent the absurdity and inequity of his childhood culture. He found the teetotaling, Baptist, Sunday School world to be banal, inane, and shot through with moral contradiction—especially the blatant racism in Tuscaloosa in the 1950s. As a great reader and student of history, my father came to appreciate a more sophisticated moral culture. He became an admirer of William Wilberforce and of classical British liberalism; when he had children, he would push them into literature and history rather than participating in the parochial culture of small-town Alabama.

My dad learned virtue by living with his father, not by listening to him. In my case, the situation was reversed: I went to boarding school and lived apart from my family. My peers rather than my parents brought me to maturity. I learned my unconscious moral habits from the youth culture of the '80s and not through the work ethic of my postwar parents.

Unlike my father, who unknowingly learned the virtues at his father's side, my social world was largely devoid of virtue-building activity. My memories of childhood include a lot of loneliness, isolation, and a sense of inadequacy. The world of rock culture offered me the hope of purpose and belonging: My idol at age thirteen was Eddie van Halen.

People, including parents, act mostly from unconscious habit rather than deliberate reflection. That is not a problem when culture instills good habits. My father learned good habits as a child without conscious reflection: For all the serious problems in 1950s Tuscaloosa, there was a sense in the air that virtue mattered—even if it had racial blind spots. But between my father's childhood and mine, culture and the American economy changed significantly. I grew up in a very different world from my father's, and that would have a significant impact on how I would eventually approach parenting.

* * *

It took me years to understand these dynamics, and my Presbyterian background was not much help. What I remember about religion as a child was the constant exhortation "to be born again," "to receive Christ," and "to invite Jesus into your heart." I received instruction in biblical morality but practiced very few regular virtue-building activities. Jill's background also offered her relatively few opportunities to learn virtue.

Jill and I struggled for years watching our kids suffer while we bickered over parenthood and fell into mutual suspicion. It was in this desperation that Jill prayed to St. Thérèse, "Save our little family!" But we also began to watch the families that worked, and we spent time with the Dominican sisters, appreciating what they were trying to bring to our children.

You do not have to be a Catholic to raise virtuous children. My grandfather was proof of that. But my grandfather was virtuous despite his Baptist faith, not because of it. In fact, his whole life put the lie to the notions of "faith alone" and "Scripture alone." He had a practical wisdom born of experience, and he learned virtue through hard practice, not because of an altar call.

Grandfather was virtuous in part because of the virtues unconsciously embedded in his culture and upbringing. But where is that culture today? Jill and I were not going to acquire virtues we never had by resurrecting a culture we never knew. There was no culture of personal virtue in our sex, drugs, and rock 'n' roll world of the 1980s.

But there is one moral community today that still extols virtue; more than that, it promises to deliver it. Even if you were deprived of my grandfather's upbringing, the Church says you can be reformed in the image of Christ through those virtue-building tools, the sacraments.

* * *

"I forgive you."

"I forgive you."

I do not remember the day, but I remember the emotion. My wife looked at me with love for the first time in years and sincerely forgave me. She stopped looking at me as a rival to her children's well-being, and I stopped looking at her as a worrywart who put up barriers to their thriving. Together, we began to look at one another as partners in a common enterprise.

We gave up our own plans and goals for our children, and we stopped trying to palliate our own emotional wounds. We instead entrusted our children to God and turned to Christ in the sacraments. And the mutual suspicion that defined our relationship for so many years has never returned.

Chapter 14

Suffering, Prayer, and Contemplation

Jill and I learned to love each other again through prayer. It was in prayer that we stopped trying to run away from our problems and instead learned how to find God in the concrete and sometimes difficult circumstances of life. Prayer opened the door to let sacramental grace flow into our lives. It all began in prayer, especially Jill's prayer.

We thought we knew all about prayer before we were Catholic, having spent thousands of hours in prayer meetings and worship services. But we did not know what the Catholic Church has to say about prayer. We did not know that prayer is a lot more than asking God for stuff. We did not know that prayer is more than praise songs and improvised expressions of gratitude to God. These are all good things, but they do not reflect the depths of Catholic prayer.

We did not know about what the Church calls "contemplation." For a Catholic, contemplation is not just meditation, nor does it require any exotic techniques. Contemplation is a way in which God draws you into the life and sufferings of Jesus. It is a way to turn away from the self and to God, allowing Christ to become the entire focus of your mind.

In 2008, Jill discovered the Catholic mystics—the great masters of contemplative prayer—and it changed her life profoundly. And because it changed her, it also changed me.

Jill would never claim that she became a deep contemplative—but something supernatural still happened to her. Through this whole new way of praying she found a whole new way of thinking about her life. The Mass and the Sacraments became meaningful to her in a way they never had been before as she began to understand what it means to identify with the suffering Christ—and then brought this to our marriage.

We both had to unlearn a lot of falsehoods about prayer. We had to break a lot of bad habits, to rid ourselves of superstitions, and to learn from the saints. But when we did, grace began to flow in abundance.

St. Alphonsus Liguori said, "He who prays will be saved; he who does not pray will not be saved." This great saint was talking about the depths of Catholic prayer. Without the proper prayer, the Faith cannot take root in the heart.

* * *

"Thank you, God, for that parking spot."

My earliest memories of prayer are of my parents turning to God to meet the most mundane demands of life. My mother would ask God for a parking spot. We would pray to do well on tests and to get over colds. We always thanked God for the food on our table. I prayed once that God would let me win a wrestling match against a grammar school rival. At my request, my dad once prayed that I would get a girlfriend.

There is nothing wrong with this kind of prayer; indeed, Scripture tells us to "pray at all times in the Spirit, with all prayer and supplication" (Eph. 6:18). Jesus also told us to pray for daily bread. When we pray often for our daily needs, it teaches us gratitude and reliance upon God.

But there is a danger in purely petitionary prayer, which is that we will turn to God only for what we want or only what pleases us. This is a form of superstition, and Sacred Scripture condemns it. St. James warns against those who pray only "to spend it on your passions" (James 4:3).

Growing up, I thought of prayer simply as petition, and I often asked God for things to spend on my pleasures. Worse, I saw little reason to ask for anything else. I certainly did not think of prayer as a place to reform my moral life or to embrace suffering. I was sure I was going to Heaven. Why would I need to embrace suffering? I wanted only to avoid it.

* * *

There are peculiar pitfalls for Catholics in prayer, and it is very easy to misunderstand it. There are even forms of superstition to which Catholics are especially susceptible.

One danger in Catholic prayer is that the Church's tradition of prayer is just so extensive. There are so many prayers that have been composed through the ages that it can be impossible to focus on any one thing at any one time. I have known Catholics who are so accustomed to standardized prayers that they are uncomfortable praying spontaneously.

Non-Catholics sometimes think that formulaic prayers are necessarily a bad thing, but this isn't true. Jesus *commanded* us to use formulaic prayer: The Lord's Prayer is as formulaic as it gets. The Psalms are also very formulaic and repetitive, and they made up the official prayer book for the early apostolic Church.

The danger is not in the existence of formulas but in the assumption that bare recitation is enough. This is something that Jesus warned about: "In praying do not heap up empty phrases as the Gentiles do; for they think that they will be heard for their many words" (Matt. 6:7). The Old Testament prophets of Baal give us almost a perfect illustration of prayer badly done (see 1 Kings 18:20ff.). They are the epitome of the worst of superstition: meaningless repetition, self-harm, and frenzied emotion.

Catholics make use of many popular devotions that have evolved over the centuries. These are good but, like anything, can be dangerous if abused. Many of these devotions are encrusted with legends or stories promising specific cures and graces if the rituals are performed properly. We find instructions, for instance, to say certain novenas to fulfill certain specific desires or to wear special items to protect us from harm.

There is nothing wrong with following such prescriptions—if they are taken properly. In fact, the Church encourages us to make use of popular devotions. But we would move into superstition if we imagined that prayer were nothing more than a magic formula.

Catholic theologians and spiritual writers have warned against superstition for centuries. In the fourth century, St. Augustine denounced the rampant superstition in Christian congregations. In his book *On Christian Doctrine*, St. Augustine explains the danger in ascribing supernatural power to an object simply because of convention, rather than because of something inherent in its nature:

> For it is one thing to say, "If you drink the juice of this herb, your stomach will not hurt," and quite another to say, "If you hang this herb around your neck, your stomach will not hurt." ... [Thus,] the question often remains as to whether the thing ... is valid because of the force of nature, in which case it is to be used freely, or is valid because of some signifying convention, in which case the Christian should avoid it.[33]

[33] Augustine, *On Christian Doctrine*, trans. D.W. Robertson (New York: Macmillan, 1958), 65.

There is even a danger of superstition in Holy Mass. The *Catechism of the Catholic Church* remarks:

> Superstition is the deviation of religious feeling and of the practices this feeling imposes. It can even affect the worship we offer the true God, e.g., when one attributes an importance in some way magical to certain practices otherwise lawful or necessary. To attribute the efficacy of prayers or of sacramental signs to their mere external performance, apart from the interior dispositions that they demand, is to fall into superstition (see Matt. 23:16–22). (2111)

The Church has always taught that valid sacraments convey grace, but also that they do not impose that grace upon us without our free cooperation. While the sacraments are a lot more than signs and symbols, symbolism is part of their value, as they work in part by conveying truths to our minds and hearts. But our minds and hearts must cooperate with what is signified before the grace of the sacrament begins to flow. If we lack faith and charity, we gain nothing from the sacraments.

Francis de Sales is another saint and Doctor of the Church who warned against the danger of Catholic superstition. His great book *Introduction to the Devout Life* begins by dismissing superstitious forms of religious life. True devotion, he teaches, is not found specifically in the multiplication of prayers, fasting, self-denial, or gifts to the poor. True devotion, rather, is founded in love toward God and neighbor:

> All true and living devotion presupposes the love of God;—and indeed it is neither more nor less than a very real love of God, though not always of the same kind; for that Love, one while shining on the soul, we call grace, which makes us acceptable to His Divine Majesty;—when it strengthens

> us to do well, it is called Charity;—but when it attains its fullest perfection, in which it not only leads us to do well, but to act carefully, diligently, and promptly, then it is called Devotion.[34]

When Jill and I first became Catholic, many of these distinctions were lost on us. Our prayer life to that point had been mixed: We had moments of grace and charity, but we also experienced a great deal of superstition, emotion, and egotism. What started us on the path to real growth in our Catholic life was a transformation in our experience of prayer.

The Catholic Church saved my marriage by teaching us how to think about marriage, parenthood, and the moral life. The Church saved *us* by offering us grace in the sacraments. She saved *us* by proposing the saints as models of holiness. She saved *us* by sending wonderful priests to accompany us in our struggles, religious who served our family, and friends in the Faith who loved us. But none of that would have worked if the Church had not also taught us how to pray.

* * *

Jill's experience in the confessional with Fr. Angelus marked the turning point in our marriage. There was no doubt in my mind about that. But at the time, I didn't really understand why. I just knew she went into the confessional filled with despair and bitterness, and came out a changed person.

In the confessional, Jill received forgiveness, peace of conscience, encouragement, and hope for the future. But how? What was the precise nature of the hope she received? Did she think that

[34]Francis de Sales, *Introduction to the Devout Life*, ed. W. H. Hutchings (London: Rivingtons, 1882), 2–3.

life would be utterly transformed? Did she think her husband would change? Did she think her material conditions would change?

Fr. Angelus promised her none of these things. He did not tell her that God would wave a magic wand and make her problems go away. He did not promise her health, wealth, or even personal satisfaction. What Fr. Angelus offered her was a new perspective on her past and present circumstances and a new way to think about the likelihood of future suffering.

Most people spend their lives trying to run away from suffering. We will do almost anything to avoid it. Whole civilizations have been constructed around the ideal of eliminating suffering. In the Buddhist tradition, the core doctrine is that life is suffering and that the Buddha offers the path to liberation from suffering.

Catholics are also concerned with the problem of suffering. For centuries, the Church has combated suffering by building up hospitals, schools, and relief agencies. Catholics were also the first public advocates for human rights, justice, and peace. In the ancient world, Catholics were the only people who would go out of their way to care for strangers. Jesus' most celebrated parable—of the good Samaritan—embodied the Catholic ideal for the elimination of suffering.

Even so, the Church has always known and taught that some suffering can never be eliminated. Unlike Buddhists, Catholics do not think the whole point of life is to eliminate suffering. The point of life is ennobling spiritual friendship with God and neighbor. We cannot possibly achieve that goal without a willingness to embrace suffering—even the suffering of an unhappy marriage.

* * *

Many people are willing to suffer for the sake of some expected good. Soldiers give their lives in defense of their country. Parents give up pleasures now for their children's future benefit. Artists, musicians, and students give hours of tedious study and practice to master skills and to acquire knowledge. But the Catholic Faith asks something of us that is far more mysterious and more difficult: The Church asks us willingly to endure some suffering *even when there is no promise of tangible benefit*. But what She does promise is that this suffering can be redeemed beyond time and space and in ways we cannot presently understand.

In the introduction to this book, I mentioned that some parts of Catholic tradition are applicable to anyone, but other parts cannot be accepted without embracing the whole Catholic worldview. The Catholic teaching on suffering is one of those parts that does not make sense without belief in God, the Church, the sacraments, and the Catholic plan of salvation. It lies right at the mysterious heart of Catholic spirituality. But it is also the Catholic teaching that is most sublime and elevating, and that has the greatest capacity to transform our lives.

How can willingly endured suffering radically transform our lives? Answering this question takes us into the core of the Catholic Faith—into the Eucharist, the communion of saints, penance, purgatory, indulgences, and all those beliefs and practices that non-Catholics find so difficult. It also carries us straight to Christ and to salvation.

Jesus said, "Whoever does not bear his own cross and come after me, cannot be my disciple" (Luke 14:27). To appreciate fully the Catholic teaching on suffering, we must understand why Jesus died on the Cross and how the benefits of His death and Resurrection are communicated to us. We must understand how our suffering, willingly and faithfully endured, connects us to Christ. In so doing, we will also better understand our connection to Our Lady of Sorrows, the Blessed Virgin Mary, who also willingly endured suffering. She is the model Christian, who prayed, "Be it done to me according to thy word" (see Luke 1:38).

* * *

Why did Christ die? We need to understand the depth of Catholic doctrine on this subject to appreciate the Church's teaching on suffering. One of the most common questions I have gotten in my work in Catholic radio is this: "Since Jesus paid the penalty for my sins on the Cross, why should I have to do anything to be saved? Why should I have to suffer?"

Protestants and Catholics have very different ideas about the death of Christ, and the problem is that many, and perhaps most, people know only the Protestant doctrine. Growing up Protestant, I learned that my sin moved God to anger and that His wrath had to be appeased by blood sacrifice. My church taught that the Crucifixion was a vicarious punishment: God agreed to punish an innocent victim, treating Him as if He were guilty of my offense. In exchange, if I had faith, I would get off scot-free. All my sins are "paid for," and there is nothing left for me to do.

Protestants use the theological term "imputation" to describe this exchange: God "imputes" my sin to Christ, treating Him as if He were guilty, and He in turn "imputes" Christ's righteousness to the believer, treating him as if he were innocent. This is the core theological difference between Protestants and Catholics, and it is what grounds the Protestant doctrine of salvation by faith alone. It is also what makes it very difficult for Protestants to appreciate the Catholic understanding of suffering.

If this is what Christ's death means, then the Catholic teaching on suffering really does seem absurd. Even if I suffer for righteousness' sake, the Protestant thinks, I can't add anything to the death of Christ. Faith alone connects me to Jesus, and Jesus has already "paid it all." Why should I bother? It is true that many Protestants have suffered heroically for their beliefs, but the *theological* dilemma remains. What can suffering do for me if I am connected to Christ by faith alone?

The Catholic Church understands the death of Christ differently. The Bible simply does not describe this ultimate moment as a vicarious punishment imposed by God. Scripture refers to the death of Christ instead as a *sacrifice* and a *ransom*, modeled after and in fulfillment of the sacrifices of the Old Testament.

The Jews did not understand the sacrifice of goats and bulls as a vicarious punishment imposed by God on a dying animal. Instead, they understood such sacrifices as opportunities for the worshipper to give up something valuable to God as a token of repentance, thanksgiving, or praise. King David said, "I will not offer burnt offerings to the LORD my God which cost me nothing" (2 Sam. 24:24).

Throughout the Old Testament, God commands animal sacrifice—but He also says that He is not *pleased* by animal sacrifice. God cares nothing about the death of an animal *per se*, but He does care for it as a token or sign of repentance, thanksgiving, or piety.

Psalm 51 expresses this relationship beautifully. The psalmist promises to offer sacrifices to God, knowing that it is the contrition of heart, and not the death of the animal, that pleases Him:

> For thou hast no delight in sacrifice;
> were I to give a burnt offering, thou wouldst not be pleased.
> The sacrifice acceptable to God is a broken spirit;
> a broken and contrite heart, O God, thou wilt not despise.
>
> Do good to Zion in thy good pleasure;
> rebuild the walls of Jerusalem,
> then wilt thou delight in right sacrifices,
> in burnt offerings and whole burnt offerings;
> then bulls will be offered on thy altar. (Ps. 51:16–19)

The real fruit of Old Testament sacrifice was the authentic spirit of contrition, thanksgiving, and love into which the believer entered. The Old Testament sacrifices also foreshadowed the ultimate sacrifice of Christ.

The heart of sacrifice is not vicarious punishment, but willingly giving up something of value. It was costly for the Jews to give up goats and bulls. *It is even more costly* to give up my pride, my lusts, or even my own self-determination. Mary gave up the right to direct her own life when she gave her *fiat* to the angel of the Lord. This is what Jesus meant when He said, "I have come ... not to do my will, but the will of him who sent me" (John 6:38).

Christ said that God sent Him to preach good news to the poor, to announce the year of the Lord's favor, and to bring the Kingdom of God—and Jesus embraced that mission, even though it would cost Him everything. He gave up the possibility of marriage, children, material possessions, and even His own life. He was "persecuted for righteousness' sake" (Matt. 5:10). The Jews and the Romans put an innocent man to death for speaking the truth.

Jesus' willing self-sacrifice was noble and pleasing to God—infinitely more so because of the righteousness and dignity of the one making the sacrifice. St. Paul explains, "He humbled himself and became obedient unto death, even death on a cross. Therefore God has highly exalted him" (Phil. 2:8–9).

The death of Christ was not a vicarious punishment that satisfied the wrath of an angry God, but the ultimate act of self-giving, of martyrdom, and of testimony to the truth for love of God and neighbor. And therefore, it was infinitely meritorious.

* * *

How does the death of Christ benefit us? If it was not a vicarious punishment imposed by God, then what does it do for me? Let's focus on three things that Scripture teaches on this subject: First,

Christ's death is an example to us; second, Christ's death merits for us the forgiveness of sins and the gift of the Spirit; and third, we die with Christ in baptism and are born again with Him to new life.

First, Christ's death is an example of suffering for what is right. St. Peter writes:

> For what credit is it, if when you do wrong and are beaten for it you take it patiently? But if when you do right and suffer for it you take it patiently, you have God's approval. For to this you have been called, because Christ also suffered for you, leaving you an example, that you should follow in his steps. (1 Pet. 2:20–21)

Second, by his heroic martyrdom, Jesus merited reward from God, which is worlds apart from the idea of vicarious punishment. What He won from God was the gift of the Holy Spirit, whom He pours out on the Church to empower our lives for holy living. Again, St. Peter explains:

> This Jesus God raised up, and of that we all are witnesses. Being therefore exalted at the right hand of God, and having received from the Father the promise of the Holy Spirit, he has poured out this which you see and hear. (Acts 2:32–33)

The third biblical teaching about the death of Christ is the most mysterious. St. Paul explains that we become members of Christ's Mystical Body through baptism. In some way that we cannot see or feel, we are joined to Him on the Cross, dying with Him and rising again with Him on the third day. Our old life dies and we are given a new life that is supernatural and powerful.

> What shall we say then? Are we to continue in sin that grace may abound? By no means! How can we who died to sin still live in it? Do you not know that all of us who

> have been baptized into Christ Jesus were baptized into his death? We were buried therefore with him by baptism into death, so that as Christ was raised from the dead by the glory of the Father, we too might walk in newness of life. (Romans 6:1–4)

The Catholic Church sees the death of Christ as a mystical sacrifice that pleases God and transforms us. When we are joined to Christ through faith and baptism, we die and rise with Him; our hearts are changed; we receive the gift of the Holy Spirit; our sins are forgiven; and we receive power to live a holy life in imitation of His. We receive salvation because we can now say, along with Jesus and His Mother, "Be it done to me according to thy word. I have come not to do my will, but the will of him who sent me."

* * *

God redeems suffering that is willingly endured for righteousness' sake. That is the message of the gospel and that is what the death of Christ means. The power of salvation that flows into us in the sacraments is the power to embrace noble suffering for the love of God.

How do we embrace that power and make it our own? Now we are coming to the real heart of Catholic prayer and the sacramental life—and the profound difference between Catholicism and other forms of Christianity. The message of the gospel is that we "become Christ." His life is not merely *imputed* to us; rather, it *becomes* ours, inwardly transforming us. And this can happen only through prayer.

The greatest, deepest, most powerful prayer of the Church is the Holy Sacrifice of the Mass. There is nothing more important. According to St. John Paul II, the Eucharist is not just the greatest thing Jesus has given us; it is the greatest thing Jesus *could* give us, since it is the gift of His very Self. Truly, the Eucharist is "the source and summit" of our faith.[35]

Understandably, converts often cite the Eucharist as the key motive for their conversion: They desire strongly to receive Christ in Holy Communion. This is also one of the chief reasons Christ instituted the Mass, so that He might be present to us in the Sacrament and received by us as food and drink for our salvation.

While there is no greater gift than to receive Christ Himself in Holy Communion, Catholic tradition says that there is something even more fundamental to the Mass than our reception of Communion, which is the truth that the Mass *is a sacrifice given to God*. This sacrifice propitiates God and brings us grace and mercy if we approach it contritely, whether we receive Communion or not.

This truth is not well understood, but it is extremely important. Like the hemorrhaging woman who touched Christ's garment, we truly touch Christ in the sacrament. But that touching does not exhaust the meaning of the Mass. Pope Benedict reflects the whole Catholic tradition when he writes, "The Eucharist draws us into Jesus' act of self-oblation. More than just statically receiving the incarnate Logos, we enter into the very dynamic of his self-giving."[36]

This matters because it should affect the disposition we bring to Mass. Do we go to Mass simply to receive something, or to make a gift of ourselves to God? Do we go with an attitude of entitlement, or of gratitude? The *Catechism* says it is superstitious to expect divine benefits from Communion if we lack this proper disposition (2111).

The Second Vatican Council explained this truth clearly:

[35]See CCC 1324; cf. Second Vatican Council, Dogmatic Constitution on the Church *Lumen Gentium* (November 21, 1964), no. 11.

[36]*Deus Caritas Est*, no. 13.

> [The faithful] should give thanks to God; by offering the Immaculate Victim, not only through the hands of the priest, but also with him, they should learn also to offer themselves; through Christ the Mediator.[37]

We can't participate properly in Mass if we have no understanding of its sacrificial structure; we can't participate fruitfully if we do not join ourselves to Christ in conversion—in the pursuit of perfection. But if we learn to offer ourselves *along with* Christ, then we become people habituated to sacrifice. That is, we become people like Christ.

Pope Pius XII wrote extensively on this topic, warning against the tendency to approach the Mass without the dynamic of conversion:

> God cannot be honored worthily unless the mind and heart turn to Him in quest of the perfect life, and ... the worship rendered to God by the Church in union with her divine Head is the most efficacious means of achieving sanctity.[38]

* * *

I met Jill in New Orleans, Louisiana, in 1990. One day under the Oak Trees in Audubon Park, when she revealed her torturous childhood to me, I had a glimpse of our lives bound together in suffering—though I had no idea what that would mean. I also saw in this girl a deep spiritual longing. I thought I could speak to that longing by introducing her to the Protestant church. This turned out to be only a beginning that started us on the path home in the Catholic Church.

[37]Second Vatican Council, Constitution on the Sacred Liturgy *Sacrosanctum Concilium* (December 4, 1963), no. 48.

[38]Pius XII, encyclical *Mediator Dei* (November 20, 1947), no. 26.

Fr. Angelus challenged Jill to look at her suffering in another way. He spoke to her of Christ and the Mass, and he showed her how to offer her sufferings along with Christ. He did not just tell her to sacrifice for the sake of her children, but also that by sacrifice she might grow closer to God, that God could redeem her suffering, and that she could find the intimacy she had longed for all her life.

Jill then threw herself into the Mass, the sacraments, and Catholic devotions with abandon. But this is not what saved her. She had abandoned herself to prayer in the past and had often cried to God in desperation, but no lasting change was effected. What changed is that she began to touch the world of contemplative prayer, which she learned from St. Teresa of Avila, the patroness of chess players.

What is contemplative prayer? Many people think that contemplation means long periods of silence, meditation, mindfulness, or exotic experiences. St. Teresa had no patience for such ideas. She despised showy or emotional piety. "God save us from pious nuns," she said.

At root, contemplative prayer is complete identification with the suffering Christ, so that one's thoughts, feelings, goals, and actions are constantly in touch with Him. The egotist lives for himself and directs all his thoughts and activities to his own interests. The contemplative lives for God.

It is possible to pray a lot and not be contemplative. We can spend long hours in meditation and not actually connect with the suffering Christ. We can slow our breathing and attain mental quiet, without purging our selfishness. We can have exotic experiences in prayer—powerful emotions, visions, and revelations—and not engage in authentic contemplation.

For the great contemplatives such as Teresa, the path to union with God is through rigorous honesty and humility. One faces the truth about one's attachments, superstitions, and selfish desires, and one abandons them to the Crucified One.

Teresa's famous prayer captures her spirituality:

> Let nothing disturb you,
> Let nothing frighten you,
> All things are passing away:
> God never changes.
> Patience obtains all things
> Whoever has God lacks nothing;
> God alone suffices.

Jill devoured the works of St. Teresa, studying her life and seeking to imitate her prayer and her virtues. What she learned from Teresa was not an *abstract* theology, but an *incarnate* theology. She saw a life utterly transformed by the gospel. She found a woman who could find God in absolutely anything—in loss, in deprivation, and in loneliness.

* * *

Teresa of Avila was not married, but another great Catholic contemplative was. Anyone who experiences struggles in marriage should know about St. Rita of Cascia (1381–1457).

St. Rita married an extremely difficult man who, because he lived a vengeful life, was murdered in a vendetta. But before he died, he was converted to a sincere Catholic faith by Rita's love and devotion. Throughout all of this, Rita bore him two sons, who died of illness early in adulthood. This marriage would likely be deemed a failure by the standards of modern psychology and couples therapy, but did it fail as a Christian marriage?

I have read a few secular books on marriage and family. I've encountered the "revolutionary five-step program for thriving relationships." I've studied techniques for "harmonious, long-lasting relationships." Many of the lessons in these books are, no doubt, useful and important. There are natural principles, drawn from psychology and science, that are true, beautiful, and good and from which Catholics can learn.

But we should ask if these worldly principles are the only criteria for a successful marriage. The Church teaches that Christian marriage exists to sanctify the spouses and to bring them to God. As a sacrament, marriage is successful if it leads to salvation. St. Paul wrote to the Ephesians:

> Husbands, love your wives, as Christ loved the church and gave himself up for her, that he might sanctify her, having cleansed her by the washing of water with the word, that he might present the church to himself in splendor, without spot or wrinkle or any such thing, that she might be holy and without blemish. (Eph. 5:25–27)

Spouses must love one another as Christ loved the Church—and for the Church He suffered torture and execution. He died for those who *did not* love Him back, for those who had abandoned and denied Him.

St. Rita lived in a world consumed with ritualized vengeance. Every slight or grievance had to be answered by inflicting the same indignity on one's enemies. Following this practice, a rival family ultimately murdered Rita's husband. Naturally, the dead man's brother urged Rita's children to take up the vendetta to avenge their father. But Rita took another path: Instead of pleading her legitimate grievance, she chose instead to forgive freely. She publicly absolved the murderers of their crime, ending the vendetta. The cycle of violence and discord was broken.

Rita became a patron saint of troubled marriages because she embraced the true meaning of Christian marriage: dying to oneself and embracing suffering to bring one's spouse and children to God.

It paid off. Rita's patient endurance finally won her husband for the Faith: He died reconciled to the Church.

Rita's holiness was the fruit of an intense life of contemplative prayer. Like Rita, we can embrace a life of suffering only if we have a powerful inner life. Otherwise we will succumb to the culture of vendetta, clinging to grievance. Rita also shows us that a life of prayer is not world-denying, but world-transforming. She did through prayer and holiness what all the politics of the day could not do. She brought peace.

* * *

Is it possible to live a contemplative life while married? If we have the wrong idea about contemplation, we might think we have to run straightaway to the monastery. If contemplation is simply sitting for long hours in silence to attain mental quiet, then no one who is married with small children could be a contemplative.

Some people, of course, are called to live a life of monastic seclusion to give themselves exclusively to God in prayer. Monks who have that vocation will be contemplatives *as monks*. But married people can be contemplatives if they learn to be contemplatives *as spouses*. The goal is the same for both: to live profoundly for God. But the path is different because the vocation is different.

Jill and I lived for many years thinking we could find our sanctity only in some activity other than marriage itself: Marriage was simply the condition that facilitated our "real" calling. I used to think I would find my sanctity through teaching, and Jill thought she could find sanctity in foreign missions. But our great contemplative "revelation" was that we could find our sanctity specifically and directly through marriage. We discovered that marriage could be a contemplative vocation.

* * *

The revolution in my marriage came when my wife adopted a contemplative perspective on family life. She stopped trying to run away from pain and trying to insulate her family against every kind of risk. Instead, she saw that all the pains, trials, and joys of family life were the precise means that God gave her to transform her life into something supernatural.

Sacraments take everyday things, such as water, oil, bread, and wine, and turn them into vehicles of grace and transcendence. The sacrament of marriage takes the everyday life of a man and a woman, with all its difficulty and messiness, and turns it into something supernatural. But you cannot receive the grace of the sacrament if you do not embrace what it symbolizes: Christ dying on the Cross to bring His spouse—the Church—to God. That is the secret to a contemplative marriage.

When I first wanted to become Catholic, my wife was skeptical. She said, "David, you've read this in books, but that is not how Catholics live." There was some truth in that criticism. Many Catholics do not live the truth that they profess, just as I did not live the truth that I professed. But when Jill embraced the Faith, she began *to live* the Faith that I had only professed.

My wife is a better person than I am. She is purer of heart and more single-minded in her pursuit of goodness. She is humbler and meeker. She hungers and thirsts more for righteousness and is more willing to be persecuted for righteousness' sake. From the time we met, she always inspired me to live my own beliefs more faithfully. I have always done a lot of talking about the faith. When Jill changed, I began to see what it looked like when people live it.

Chapter 15

Catholic Marriage: The Treasure Buried in a Field

In 1930, the Anglican Church's Lambeth Conference resulted in a statement that made a seismic shift in Christian thinking and practice by opening the door to allowing contraception and allowing remarriage after divorce. Pope Pius XII knew this required a response to let the world know that the Catholic Church had not and would not follow suit. The result was *Casti Connubii*, a wise and beautiful encyclical letter about Christian marriage.

The pope reaffirmed the Church's opposition to divorce and to birth control, but he also acknowledged that these standards are difficult. The Holy Father did not offer an easy solution; on the contrary, he freely admitted that many Catholics find them impossible. The fault, however, does not lie with God *but with us*. Pius cited the Council of Trent, which teaches that God never demands the impossible of us: He always supplies the necessary grace.

If God supplies the grace, then why do some Catholics find the moral demands of marriage to be impossible? The pope's answer is astonishing for its realism and honesty. They find it impossible, he says, because they do not cooperate with grace. They do not live the faith generously. They are unwilling to sacrifice. If they do not do everything in their power—if they select only those parts of the Faith they like, or if they do not give themselves to prayer and the sacraments—then the grace of matrimony will be an unused talent hidden in the field (see Matt. 25:14–30).

The pope explains:

> Nevertheless, since it is a law of divine Providence in the supernatural order that men do not reap the full fruit of the Sacraments which they receive after acquiring the use of reason unless they cooperate with grace, the grace of matrimony will remain for the most part an unused talent hidden in the field unless the parties exercise these supernatural powers and cultivate and develop the seeds of grace they have received. If, however, doing all that lies with their power, they cooperate diligently, they will be able with ease to bear the burdens of their state and to fulfill their duties. By such a sacrament they will be strengthened, sanctified and in a manner consecrated.[39]

Catholics who reject Church teaching and do not vigorously practice their Faith simply should not expect grace from the sacrament. It may sound harsh, but they should not be surprised if their marriages fail. On the other hand, Catholics who believe the Church and practice their Faith can be confident that God will supply the necessary grace.

What is necessary in order to cooperate with the grace offered in the sacrament of matrimony? This is something that Pope John Paul II wrote about extensively. In his apostolic exhortation *Familiaris Consortio*, he explains that couples must accept and follow Church teaching on human sexuality, prayer, and the sacraments. He writes:

[39] *Casti Connubii*, no. 41.

> There is no doubt that these conditions [for receiving the grace] must include persistence and patience, humility and strength of mind, filial trust in God and in His grace, and frequent recourse to prayer and to the sacraments of the Eucharist and of Reconciliation. Thus strengthened, Christian husbands and wives will be able to keep alive their awareness of the unique influence that the grace of the sacrament of marriage has on every aspect of married life, including therefore their sexuality: the gift of the Spirit, accepted and responded to by husband and wife, helps them to live their human sexuality in accordance with God's plan and as a sign of the unitive and fruitful love of Christ for His Church. (33)

Jill and I didn't know the grace "hidden in a field" that God had already given us in baptism, and we didn't know the grace we could have through the sacrament of matrimony. As a result, we did not cooperate with grace, and we did not live authentic married love for many years.

Our marriage began to heal when we came to appreciate the nature and purpose of that love. This drove us, in turn, to seek grace through the sacraments. Married love does not exist for the purpose of romantic gratification. Married love exists "to lead the spouses to God" and to strengthen them in the "sublime office of being a mother or a father."[40]

* * *

I have a devout and wonderful Catholic friend who, like me, is a convert to the Church. Also like me, he came to Catholicism after a period of intense theological scrutiny and critical analysis.

[40]*Gaudium et Spes*, no. 48.

I asked him years after his conversion how being Catholic had affected his life. I expected him to answer with a deeply abstract and theological answer about something like doctrinal certainty or religious knowledge. But instead he spoke about his marriage: "I could not have imagined the effect that Catholic faith would have on my marriage. I could not have imagined how I would come to regard my wife with so much more dignity."

Jill once told me that Catholics were mean and unspiritual. Catholicism might look good on paper, she thought, but it never worked out in real life. And there is real truth in this criticism. There are many Catholics who do not cooperate with grace, who do not have faith, and who make little attempt to follow Church teaching. I have had fellow Catholics who advised me to avoid confession, to disbelieve Church teaching about marriage and sex, and even to divorce my wife.

There were many times in my marriage when what sustained me most of all was the example of my parents. Though my parents were not Catholic, they lived the most important Catholic truth about marriage better than many Catholics do: They were dead set against divorce, no matter what. Burn your parachute; hang on like mad; and do whatever it takes to stick in there. Without that example, I do not know if I would have made it.

Inspired by my parents, I had to look deeper and deeper to find the grace necessary to live that demand. Ultimately, that search led me and my wife to the Catholic Church. It is no credit to me; I really credit my wife with having the courage and conviction to take up the Faith with both hands, to plunge into the depth of the sacraments, to embrace the Cross, and to strive for a life of contemplative prayer. She cooperated with grace, and the result was the transformation of everything.

There has been a lot of conversation recently about the Catholic doctrine on marriage, including about how strictly pastors should insist on the Church's "hard teachings." But let me tell you this: The hard teachings saved me. I did not know about nuance or mitigating circumstances. I did know that I had a moral obligation to save my marriage or die trying. Had I really believed there was any other permissible option, my marriage would not have survived—and I am so glad that my marriage survived.

Why does Christ call Christian couples to such a high standard of fidelity, even to the point of embracing the cross of suffering? The reason is that Christian marriage is no mere human contract. It is a mystical participation in the sacrificial, self-giving love of Christ for His Church (Eph. 5). It is a special vocation to holiness, an ecclesial state in the same way that priesthood or religious life is an ecclesial state. Christian marriage participates in the sacramental mission of the Church to bring Christ to the world.

> Spouses are therefore the permanent reminder to the Church of what happened on the Cross; they are for one another and for the children witnesses to the salvation in which the sacrament makes them sharers.[41]

[41] *Familiaris Consortio*, no. 13.

Appendix

In Memoriam

Fr. Angelus Shaughnessy, OFM Cap.

November 16, 1929–March 2, 2018

Fr. Angelus Shaughnessy, OFM Cap., played a unique and essential role in healing my marriage in the Catholic Church. My wife and I owe him an eternal debt of gratitude. Unfortunately, Fr. Angelus died before I could share this manuscript with him. He went to his reward at 2:15 p.m. EST on March 2, 2018, two days after the book went to the copy editor.

By God's grace and providence, I spoke to Fr. Angelus by phone four hours before his passing. I told him again how grateful we were for his priesthood, for all that God had done through him, and for the difference he had made in our lives. I told him about this book, and how much he contributed to its completion. Fr. Angelus was too weak to converse, but with his very last breaths he lifted his hands in blessing and quietly uttered his priestly benediction. It was emblematic of his entire life: He gave himself to the last in charity for the salvation of poor sinners.

Today, I can hear echoed in his life and memory the words of St. Paul: "Be imitators of me, as I am of Christ" (1 Cor. 11:1). Surely, Fr. Angelus was to us the face of Christ's mercy.

Eternal rest grant unto them, O Lord.
And let the perpetual light shine upon them.
And may the souls of all the faithful departed,
through the mercy of God, rest in peace.
Amen.

About the Author

David Anders is an educator and radio host based in Birmingham, Alabama. He hosts the popular *Called to Communion* program on the EWTN Global Catholic Network and serves as the Director of Education and Lifelong Learning for the Diocese of Birmingham. He earned a B.A. from Wheaton College, Illinois, in 1992, an M.A. from Trinity Evangelical Divinity School in 1995, and a Ph.D. from the University of Iowa in 2002.

David married Jill Susan D'Antonio in 1992, and their marriage was convalidated in the Catholic Church in 2007. Over the years, they have shared their lives with five beautiful children and a rather large number of dogs.